The Martyrs of York
by a Father of the Oratory

The Martyrs of York

Between 1535 and 1680 York was the centre of an unprecedented slaughter of English Catholics. They died for their loyalty to the Christian faith, permitted in this place since the time of Constantine, who was acclaimed Roman Emperor in York in 306AD, and which St Paulinus firmly planted here when he dedicated the first Minster to St Peter on Easter Sunday 627. Paulinus came to York as part of the mission sent by Pope St Gregory the Great to bring the Gospel to this island. The martyrs who were executed at the Knavesmire and elsewhere refused to abandon their bond with the successor of St Peter, or to the same Mass which had been celebrated by St Wilfrid, St William and countless other Catholics up until the reformation.

All of those who have been canonized or beatified by the Church as martyrs died for their faith, and not for any disloyalty to their monarch or country. In the reign of Henry VIII it became high treason to acknowledge the authority of the papacy, and under Elizabeth I priests could be hanged, drawn and quartered simply because they were priests. Others suffered the same fate for harbouring or assisting them. The example of these brave men and women should inspire us with the same deep love for the Mass and for the unity of the Church.

Of the eighty-four names listed in this booklet, four are now canonized saints, seventy-one are *beati*, four have been declared venerable and five have yet to be honoured by the Church. Included here are not only those who died in York but also others who were born in Yorkshire and who suffered for their faith elsewhere in England. There are probably more whose witness is lost to history, but in invoking the York martyrs we also seek the prayers of those whose names are now unknown to us but whose witness is already rewarded in heaven.

It is striking that only one of these seventy-five saints and beati is a woman: Saint Margaret Clitherow. She is preeminent among the martyrs of York for the devotion shown to her and she stands for those other, hidden women who, like her, risked everything for the Mass but did not end up paying the ultimate price as she did. It was a feature of the time that women were less likely to be tried and executed, and even Elizabeth I was reported to be horrified by the reports of Margaret Clitherow's torture and execution. Obviously priests were the most likely to suffer martyrdom at this time, but they would have been unable to carry out their mission at all without the devoted help of lay Catholics, both men and women.

The principal source for our information about the York martyrs is Bishop Richard Challoner's two-volume work, published in 1741: *Memoirs of Missionary Priests and other Catholicks of both Sexes who suffered Death or Imprisonment in England on account of their Religion.* Of some martyrs we know little, simply because of the secrecy in which they were compelled to work, but they show us that we all have a part to play in building up the Kingdom of God and in passing on the Gospel to generations yet to come. In reading these little accounts of the martyrs' witness may we learn to imitate their zeal, their courage and their charity.

All you holy martyrs of York – pray for us.

Blessed Henry Abbot

Born at Howden, Yorkshire
Martyred at York, 4th July, 1597 under Elizabeth I
Beatified on 15th December, 1929 by Pope Pius XI

Henry Abbot was an English layman, himself a convert from the Church of England, who was executed at York for the alleged attempt to convert someone to the Catholic Church, which had been declared an act of treason under the Penal Laws enacted under Queen Elizabeth I.

His acts are thus related by Bishop Challoner:

"A certain Protestant minister, for some misdemeanour put into York Castle, to reinstate himself in the favour of his superiors, insinuated himself into the good opinion of the Catholic prisoners, by pretending a deep sense of repentance, and a great desire of embracing the Catholic truth . . . So they directed him, after he was enlarged, to Mr. Henry Abbot, a zealous convert who lived in Holden in the same country, to procure a priest to reconcile him . . . Mr. Abbot carried him to Carlton to the house of Esquire Stapleton, but did not succeed in finding a priest. Soon after, the traitor having got enough to put them all in danger of the law, accused them to the magistrates . . . They confessed that they had explained to him the Catholic Faith, and upon this they were all found guilty and sentenced to die."

The execution was carried out by hanging, drawing and quartering.

William Allison

Died in York Castle, 1681 under Charles II

Bishop Challoner lists this priest as having been a confessor for the faith at this time, but no further information is known of him.

Blessed John Amias

Born at Wakefield, Yorkshire
Martyred at York, 16th March, 1589 under Elizabeth I
Beatified on 15th December, 1929 by Pope Pius XI

There is some doubt as to the real name of this martyr, since he may have used an alias, but in any event, a widower calling himself John Amias entered the English College at Rheims in June 1580 and was ordained priest on 25th March the following year. From there he set out, going via Paris, to England, together with another Yorkshire priest, Blessed Edmund Sykes.

We know little of Amias's mission in England, until he was seized at the house of a Mr Murton of Melling in Lancashire at the end of 1588. The priest was brought to York Castle and sentenced to hanging, drawing and quartering. At the scaffold, Amias began to address the crowd, telling them that he died for religion, not for treason. He was cut short before he could finish his speech. Blessed Robert Dalby followed him immediately to martyrdom.

Blessed William Andleby

Born at Etton, Yorkshire
Martyred at York, 4th July, 1597 under Elizabeth I
Beatified on 15th December, 1929 by Pope Pius XI

William Andleby was born into a gentry family. At 25 he went to the Netherlands to take part in the Dutch war. He visited Douai College out of curiosity and met William Allen; a discussion led to his conversion, and eventually Andleby became a Catholic priest, being ordained on 23rd March 1577, along with Ralph Sherwin. Andleby returned to England in April 1578.

At first he worked alone. According to Challoner, "For the first four years of his mission he travelled always on foot, meanly attired, and carrying with him usually in a bag his vestments and other things for saying Mass; for his labours lay chiefly among the poor, who were not shocked with such things."

Later Andleby acquired a horse, and in around 1587 he worked with another Douai priest and native of the East Riding, William Atkinson. They travelled widely from Richmond, through York, to Howden, Hemingbrough and Hull. Andleby is known to have taken his ministry to Mr Tyrwhitt's, in Lincolnshire, and also to the Catholic prisoners in Kingston upon Hull's blockhouse.

After about 20 years, he was arrested and condemned as a Catholic priest. He was executed at York with two laymen: Thomas Warcop, and Edward Fulthrop, and the priest Henry Abbot.

Robert Aske

Born at Selby, Yorkshire
Martyred at York, 12th July, 1537 under Henry VIII

Aske was the younger son of Sir Robert Aske of Aughton near Selby, a scion of an old Yorkshire family. Queen Jane Seymour was also his third cousin through the same line. All that we know of his physical appearance is that he was blind in one eye.

Aske became a lawyer, and was a Fellow at Gray's Inn. A devout man, he objected to Henry's religious reforms, particularly the Dissolution of the Monasteries. When rebellion broke out in York against Henry VIII, Aske was returning to Yorkshire from London. Not initially involved in the rebellion, he took up the cause of the locals and headed the Pilgrimage of Grace. By 10th October 1536 he had come to be regarded as their "chief captain". Most of Yorkshire, and parts of Northumberland, Durham, Cumberland and Westmorland were in revolt.

Nine thousand insurgents marched on York, where Aske arranged for the expelled monks and nuns to return to their houses; the king's tenants were driven out and religious observance resumed.

On 13th November 1536, Aske treated with the royal delegates, including the Duke of Norfolk, and received an assurance of an audience and safe passage to the king. Among the insurgents' requests was the punishment of heretical bishops and of the king's evil advisers, the recall of his anti-ecclesiastical legislation, the prosecution of his "visitors", Lee and Layton, and the holding of a parliament in the North. He travelled to London, met Henry VIII, and received promises of redress and safe passage.

As he began his journey back north, fighting broke out again. This renewed fighting allowed Henry to change his mind, and he had Robert Aske seized and brought to the Tower of London. He was convicted of high treason in Westminster and was taken back to York, where he was hanged in chains on 12th July 1537, on a special scaffold erected outside Clifford's Tower.

Blessed Thomas Atkinson

Born at Wakefield, Yorkshire
Martyred at York, 11th March, 1616 under James I
Beatified on 22nd November, 1987
by Pope St John Paul II

Thomas Atkinson was ordained priest at Rheims, and returned to England in 1588. He was well-known, especially for visiting poor Catholics, and eventually he could not safely travel by day. He always travelled by foot until, having broken his leg, he had to ride a horse. At the age of 70 he was betrayed and taken to York with his host, Mr Vavasour of Willitoft, and some members of the family.

Atkinson would neither confirm or deny that he was a priest, so as not to incriminate Mr Vavasour and his wife and children. A pair of beads and the form of an indulgence were found upon Thomas Atkinson, and he was condemned to be hanged, drawn, and quartered.

Venerable Anthony Battie

Born in Yorkshire
Martyred at York, 22nd March, 1602 under Elizabeth I
Declared Venerable in 1886 by Pope Leo XIII

Anthony Battie, or Bates, was a Yorkshire gentleman who entertained the priest, the Venerable James Harrison, in his house, and was in consequence hanged as a traitor with him in York.

Blessed Robert Bickerdike

Born at Knaresborough, Yorkshire
Martyred at York, 5th August or 8th October, 1586
under Elizabeth I
Beatified on 22nd November, 1987
by Pope St John Paul II

Robert Bickerdike was born at Low Hall, near Knaresborough, and lived at York, where he was an apprentice. In the summer of 1585 he was seen having a glass of ale with Catholic priest John Boste, and as Bickerdike had paid, this was seen by some as sufficient grounds for an arrest. There being no evident proof, he was acquitted and discharged.

On 3rd June 1586, when Francis Ingleby was being dragged on the hurdle to execution, hearing a minister's wife say: "Let us go into the Tolbooth and we shall see the traitorly thief come over on the hurdle", Bickerdike said, "No; no thief, but as true as thou art". The father of the minister's wife had Bickerdicke committed to Ousebridge Gaol. On being found not guilty, Judge Rhodes had him removed from the city gaol to the Castle and tried once more at the Lammas Assizes on the same charge. He was then condemned. He was executed at York on 5th August or 8th October 1586.

Blessed Marmaduke Bowes

Born at Ingram Grange, Yorkshire
Martyred at York, 25th November, 1585
under Elizabeth I
Beatified on 22nd November, 1987
by Pope St John Paul II

Marmaduke Bowes was a married layman of gentleman yeoman stock. He converted to the faith, but went to the Established Church often enough to keep the authorities away and to hold on to his property. Nevertheless he sheltered fugitive priests and had his children educated as Catholics.

In 1585, Blessed Marmaduke's children's tutor apostatized and denounced Bowes for hiding priests. Both he and his wife were imprisoned in York, and though Mrs Bowes was released, Marmaduke became the first layman to be executed under the new statute that made hiding priests a felony. It was said that, 'he died very willingly and professed his faith [i.e. was openly converted to Catholicism], with great repentance that he had lived in schism.'

Marmaduke Bowes was hanged alongside Blessed Hugh Taylor, one of the priests he had sheltered.

Blessed John Britton

Born at Barnsley, Yorkshire
Martyred at York, 1st April, 1598 under Elizabeth I
Beatified on 22nd November, 1987
by Pope St John Paul II

A member of the old, established Breton family, Britton was known as a zealous Catholic. He was subjected to continual vexations and persecutions, which caused him to absent himself from his wife and family for safety. As an old man, he was accused of making traitorous speeches against the Queen and condemned to death. He refused to renounce his faith, and was executed at York on 1st April 1598. He was probably the father of Dr. Matthew Britton, prefect and professor at Douai in 1599.

Blessed Edward Burden

Born in County Durham, 1540
Martyred at York, 29th November, 1588
under Elizabeth I
Beatified on 22nd November, 1987
by Pope St John Paul II

Edward Burden was an undergraduate at Trinity College, Oxford. He later travelled to Douai, where he was ordained priest in 1584. In 1586 he came to England and served the Catholics of Yorkshire. After two years he was apprehended and languished in York Castle along with another priest, Blessed Robert Dalby. Seeing him led away to trial, Burden complained, "Shall I always lie here like a beast while my brother hastens to his reward? Truly, I am unworthy of such glory as to suffer for Christ." He followed soon afterwards though, and was himself found worthy to by hanged, drawn and quartered for Christ.

Venerable Brian Cansfield

Born at Tatham, Lancashire
Martyred at York, 1645
under the Parliamentary rebellion
Declared venerable in 1886 by Pope Leo XIII

Brian Cansfield was born in Roberts Hall, Tatham, in Lancashire. He received his early education in the local school and his upbringing was Protestant. His brothers, who were Catholics, continually encouraged him to adopt their faith, which he finally did at the age of sixteen when he went to study at the English College at Saint-Omer in Flanders. Three years later, he went to the English College in Rome, but because he had decided to enter the Society of Jesus, he returned to Flanders, became a Jesuit in 1604, and was ordained when he completed his theological studies.

His desire to work for the persecuted Church was eventually fulfilled in 1618 when he returned to England. He laboured in Lancashire, Lincolnshire, Devonshire and Yorkshire where he assumed the names of Christopher Benson and Barton. For more than twenty-five years on the English mission, he converted many Protestants and strengthened the faith of countless Catholics. Like all priests on the mission, Fr Cansfield knew his arrest could happen at any time; nonetheless he did not curtail his activities. When his arrest did occur, it was a case of mistaken identity.

In 1645, the wife of a judge in Yorkshire was reconciled to the Church through an unidentified Jesuit and had given up Protestantism for Catholicism. The enraged judge ordered priest-hunters to search throughout Yorkshire for the priest and swore that he would not rest until that priest was hanged and quartered. Fr Cansfield was celebrating Mass when the priest-hunters apprehended him at the altar. He was violently struck and abused, before the jubilant judge imprisoned him at York castle. There he endured further physical abuse and by the time they discovered that he was the wrong priest and released him, Fr Cansfield's health was beyond repair because of the severe beatings, starvation and the dampness of his prison cell.

Fr Cansfield stayed with his Jesuit brethren after his release, hoping to recover but he died a few days later. He was sixty-three and had been a Jesuit for forty-one years.

Blessed Edmund Catherick

Born in Lancashire, c.1605
Martyred at York, 13th April, 1642 under Charles I
Beatified on 15th December, 1929 by Pope Pius XI

Edmund Catherick was descended from the Catholic family Catherick of Carlton in the north riding of Yorkshire. Educated at Douai College, he was ordained in the same institution, and about 1635 went out to the English mission where he began his seven years' ministry, which closed with his death. During this time he was known under the alias Huddleston, which was probably his mother's maiden name.

Apprehended in the North Riding, near Watlas, Catherick was brought by pursuivants before Justice Dodsworth, a connection by marriage - possibly an uncle. It was through admissions made to Dodsworth, under the guise of friendship, that Catherick was convicted. He was arraigned at York and condemned to death together with Blessed John Lockwood.

The execution was stayed by the King, Charles I, for a short time, but he finally signed the warrant and it was carried out during his presence at the King's Manor in York. Catherick and Lockwood were dragged through the streets of York on a hurdle to the place of execution and hanged, drawn, and quartered. Catherick was much encouraged on the scaffold by the example of his fellow-martyr, the elderly priest John Lockwood. Before being hanged, Catherick prayed for the King, Queen and their children, "that God in His mercy would shower down His blessings upon them, and send a right understanding betwixt His Majesty and his parliament." Then he went on to pray for and forgive his persecutors, especially Mr Dodsworth. Catherick's head was placed on Micklegate Bar, and what remained of the body was buried at Toft Green and later taken to Downside Abbey.

Blessed James Claxton

Born in Yorkshire
Martyred in Middlesex, 28th August, 1588
under Elizabeth I
Beatified on 15th December, 1929 by Pope Pius XI

James Claxton journeyed to the continent to study for the priesthood, receiving his seminary education at the English College of Rheims. Following his ordination, Claxton returned to England in 1582 to begin serving the country's Catholic population persecuted by the Protestant regime of Queen Elizabeth I. Within three years of his return, he was arrested and imprisoned. In 1585, he was banished from England for being a priest, but determined not to abandon the English faithful, Claxton secretly re-entered the country. He was soon discovered by the authorities, who after capturing him put him on trial.

James Claxton was sentenced to death for being a priest and for defying the banishment order. He suffered execution by drawing and quartering together with the young Minim friar Blessed Thomas Felton on 28th August, 1588 between Branford and Hounslow, Middlesex.

Saint Margaret Clitherow

Born at York, 1556
Martyred at York, 25th March, 1586 under Elizabeth I
Beatified on 15th December, 1929 by Pope Pius XI
Canonized on 25th October, 1970 by Pope St Paul VI

St Margaret Clitherow is one of the best known and loved of the English Martyrs. Margaret Middleton was born in York in 1556. In 1571 she married a prosperous butcher, John Clitherow. She became a Catholic in 1574.

At a time when it was held to be an act of treason to be a Catholic priest in England or to shelter a priest, Margaret had Mass celebrated above the family's house and shop in the Shambles. She also ran a small school to teach the Catholic Faith to children.

In 1586 her activities were betrayed to the authorities. When charged, Margaret refused to plead. She did not want to expose her family, friends or the children in her school to the risks involved in giving evidence in a trial: they may have betrayed others; they might have denied their faith in public.

The penalty for refusing to plead was being crushed to death. It was expected that the victim, in the absence of other evidence, might betray herself under the torture. Margaret suffered this fate on 25th March, 1586. It was Good Friday and the Feast of the Annunciation. She prayed aloud but gave nothing away.

Margaret Clitherow had three children. Her son Henry Clitherow went abroad to train as a priest and returned to work on the English Mission.

The shrine of St Margaret Clitherow is located in The Shambles and Mass is celebrated there every Saturday at 10am. St Margaret's hand is venerated at the Bar Convent.

Blessed Alexander Crow

Born at Howden, Yorkshire, c.1550
Martyred at York, 30th November 1586/7, 1587
under Elizabeth I
Beatified on 22nd November, 1987
by Pope St John Paul II

Alexander Crow was a cobbler, but in his twenties he travelled to Rheims and was ordained priest in 1584. He returned to England, working in the north of England, but then was arrested while baptizing the baby of Cecily Garnet at South Duffield. Brought to York he was hanged, drawn and quartered 'being about the year of thirty-five', which may have been 1586 or 1587.

Bishop Richard Challoner in 'Memoirs of the Missionary Priests', relates the following story about Blessed Alexander Crow:

"He was in a cell with another Catholic prisoner who later reported on the vigil Father Crow kept. He wanted to stay awake and pray, preparing himself for the horrors of being hanged, drawn, and quartered. In the midst of his prayers, however, he was tempted by the devil, who told him he would never be a martyr and never enjoy heaven, but be kept in prison forever and go to hell. The "ugly monster" told him to kill himself rather than endure such lingering punishment. Father Crow kept fighting him off, but the "horrid figure" kept harassing him. Suddenly a vision of St. John the Evangelist and the Blessed Virgin Mary appeared to Father Crow, casting the demon away and telling him, "Begone from hence, thou cursed creature! Thou hast no part in this servant of Christ, who will shed his blood tomorrow for his Lord, and will enter into his joy." Crow received great spiritual consolation and rejoiced that he would indeed be a martyr the next day."

On the scaffold, however, the devil returned and knocked Father Crow off the ladder even before the noose was placed around his neck; the crowd gathered for the execution thought he was trying to kill himself. He told them that he was not, mounted the ladder again and after "exhorting them to the Catholic faith" and "passing through the usual course of the ordinary butchery, he gloriously finished his career, and went to enjoy his God forever."

Blessed Robert Dalby

Born at Hemingbrough, Yorkshire
Martyred at York, 16th March, 1589 under Elizabeth I
Beatified on 15th December, 1929 by Pope Pius XI

Robert Dalby (sometimes called Drury) was a minster of the Established Church, but converted to the Catholic Faith and went to Rheims in 1586 to study for the priesthood. Upon ordination in April 1588 he set out for England, but was almost immediately arrested upon his landing at Scarborough and imprisoned in York Castle.

Blessed Robert, together with Blessed John Amias, were led out to the Knavesmire, where they prostrated themselves in prayer before the execution. Dalby had to watch Amias being hanged, drawn and quartered immediately before him, but he went without hesitation to his own death. Those who venerated the bodies of the two priests reported many miracles.

Blessed William Dean

Born at Linton-in-Craven, Yorkshire
Martyred at Mile End, London, 28th August, 1588 under Elizabeth I
Beatified on 15th December, 1929 by Pope Pius XI

William Dean went to school in Leeds and Clitheroe, before becoming a sizar at Magdalene College, Cambridge in 1575 and then a pensioner at Gonville & Caius in 1577. He then headed for the English College at Rheims, and was ordained priest at Soissons on 21st December 1581, along with two other future martyrs: George Haydock and Robert

Nutter. At just the same time, the news of St Edmund Campion's martyrdom reached the College.

Dean said his first Mass on 9th January and left for England on the 25th. In 1585 he was banished, along with a number of other priests, and deposited on the coast of Normandy. He knew that death awaited him if he were apprehended a second time, but he quickly returned to the Mission. Three years later he was arrested in the midst of anti-Catholic fever, following the failure of the Spanish Armada. Twenty-seven Catholics were executed that year, and six new gibbets were erected in London, said to be at the instigation of the bloodthirsty Earl of Leicester.

Dean died alongside Blessed Henry Webley, a layman, originally from Gloucestershire, who was condemned for relieving and assisting him. 28th August 1588 was the day of seven martyrdoms. At his execution Dean tried to speak to the people, "but his mouth was stopped by some that were in the cart, in such a violent manner that they were like to have prevented the hangman of his wages".

Blessed Francis Dickinson

Born at Otley, Yorkshire, October 1564
Martyred at Rochester, Kent, 13th April, 1590
under Elizabeth I
Beatified on 15th December, 1929 by Pope Pius XI

Francis was born in Otley and christened at Otley Parish Church on 28th October 1564. Nothing is known of his early life, but in 1582, at the age of seventeen, he entered the English College in Rheims. He was ordained at Soissons on 18th March 1589 and returned to England in November of that year. He was captured along with another priest, Miles Gerard, when the ship on which they were travelling to England met a violent storm and was shipwrecked on the Kent coast. Upon refusing to swear allegiance to the Queen, Francis was sent to London and committed to Bridewell Prison.

During this time he was tortured in an attempt to obtain a self-incriminating confession. The date and place of his trial are unknown, however, he was taken to Rochester and there hanged, drawn and quartered on 13th April 1590. Francis had been a priest for just over one year and, at the age of twenty-five, was one of the youngest Douai martyrs.

Blessed George Douglas

Born in Edinburgh, c.1540
Martyred at York, 9th September, 1587 under Elizabeth I
Beatified on 22nd November, 1987
by Pope St John Paul II

Originally from Scotland, George Douglas was a schoolmaster in Rutland, who converted to Catholicism and went to France around 1556, where he was later ordained priest in the Cathedral of Notre Dame, Paris in 1574. He then came to the north of England, disguised in a coarse, canvas doublet and hose and also ministered in the East Midlands. After being arrested a first time, Douglas was released, but then he was captured again at Ripon and found guilty in York of "persuading the Queen's subjects to popery" and executed by hanging, drawing and quartering as a traitor. Witnesses reported that he showed great fortitude.

Blessed John Duckett

Born at Sedbergh, Yorkshire, 1603
Martyred at Tyburn, London, 7th September, 1644
under the Parliamentary rebellion
Beatified on 15th December, 1929 by Pope Pius XI

John Duckett was the son of the Protestants James Duckett and his wife Frances Girlington. The boy was baptized after a long delay on 24th February 1614. He was educated at Sedbergh School and brought up a Protestant like his parents but was received into the Catholic Church by the priest Andrew North. At the age of about thirty he entered the English College, Douai, arriving on 1st March 1633; he was ordained a priest by the Archbishop of Cambrai in 1639 and was then sent to study for three years at the College of Arras in Paris.

Duckett is said to have had an extraordinary gift of prayer, and as a student would spend whole nights in contemplation. After Paris it came time to embark on the English mission, but on his way he spent two months in retreat under the direction of his uncle, John Duckett, prior of the Charterhouse at Nieupoort. Once he arrived in England around Christmas 1643, Duckett worked largely in the North and laboured for about a year in Durham. It was in the time of the Civil War and he was seized only a few months later, on 2nd July 1644, near Wolsingham in the neighbourhood of Lanchester, County Durham, while on his way to baptize two children. Taken to Sunderland, he was examined by a Parliamentary Committee of sequestrators and placed in irons. He admitted he was a priest and so was taken to London with the Jesuit Ralph Corby, arrested about the same time near Newcastle-upon-Tyne. They were both confined in Newgate, where they were the cause of crowds of Catholics gathering. On these and on others who encountered them they made an impression by their cheerfulness and sanctity. He was brought to trial on 4th September and given the inevitable and terrible sentence of hanging, drawing and quartering the day after. It was carried out at Tyburn in London on 7th September 1644. His fate was shared by the Jesuit Blessed Ralph Corby.

Blessed George Errington

Born at Hurst Castle, Northumberland, c.1554
Martyred at York, 29th November, 1596
under Elizabeth I
Beatified on 22nd November, 1987
by Pope St John Paul II

George Errington was a member of the Catholic gentry and came from Hurst Castle in Northumberland. He was imprisoned for taking part in an uprising and held in York Castle along with William Knight and William Gibson, both of whom were Catholics.

Along with them was a genuine felon, who was also an Anglican minister. In order to secure his own release he tricked the Catholics into thinking that he had an interest in converting to the Faith, and then betrayed them. Convicted of treason for this under the Penal Laws enacted under Queen Elizabeth I, Errington was condemned to death. For this he suffered hanging, drawing and quartering at York on 29th November 1596. Two years before his own death, George Errington had ridden with the priest John Boste on his last journey from York to Durham.

Blessed John Finglow

Born at Barnby, near Howden, Yorkshire
Martyred at York, 8th August, 1586 under Elizabeth I
Beatified on 22nd November, 1987
by Pope St John Paul II

John Finglow (or Fingley) was a sizar of Gonville and Caius College, Cambridge from 1573. He arrived at the English College in Rheims in February 1580 and was ordained priest on Lady Day the following year. The next month he was sent on the English mission, where he laboured for souls for the next five years.

On being arrested, Finglow was imprisoned in the Ousebridge Kidcote, York in extreme discomfort, somewhat alleviated by a fellow prisoner, and then tried for being a Catholic priest and reconciling English subjects to the Catholic Church. He was executed by hanging, drawing and quartering.

Saint John Fisher

Born at Beverley, Yorkshire, c.19th October, 1469
Martyred at Tower Hill, London, 22nd June, 1535
under Henry VIII
Beatified on 29th December, 1886 by Pope Leo XIII
Canonized on 19th May, 1935 by Pope Pius XI

John Fisher was the son of a Beverley merchant, and was educated at the ancient Beverley Grammar School, before studying at Michaelhouse, Cambridge. He was ordained priest in 1491, and became a fellow of his college as well as vicar of Northallerton, Yorkshire until 1494. He was then made a Proctor of Cambridge University and became confessor to Margaret Beaufort, the mother of King Henry VII. It was under Fisher's influence that Lady Margaret founded Christ's and St John's Colleges in Cambridge, and endowed the Lady Margaret Professorships of Divinity in both Oxford and Cambridge, which exist to this day. John Fisher was the first Lady Margaret Professor in Cambridge, he was elected Chancellor of the University in 1504 (which post he held until his death) and from 1505-8 was the President of Queens' College.

John Fisher was known by scholars throughout Europe for his learning, his virtue and his austerity. Yet it is as a bishop – a pastor of the Lord's flock – that he can most clearly be seen as a saint. He was made Bishop of Rochester in 1505, the poorest see in England, and remained faithful to this calling for the rest of his life.

Fisher acted as tutor to the young Prince Henry, but when this prince reigned as Henry VIII, the saint could not but take the part of his wronged wife, Catherine of Aragon, and to defend the indissolubility of Christian marriage and the primacy of the papacy. When John Fisher refused to take an oath recognizing the king's marriage to Anne Boleyn in April 1534, he was imprisoned in the Tower of London (at the same time as St Thomas More) under harsh conditions. He was allowed no priest to visit him right until the end.

In May 1535 Pope Paul III created John Fisher Cardinal Priest of San Vitale, in the hope that this would ease his treatment. On the contrary however, this enraged King Henry, who declared that by the time the cardinal's hat arrived, he would have no head on which to wear it. On 17th

June the Cardinal was convicted of treason and of denying that the king was supreme head of the Church of England.

St John was to be beheaded, just like his namesake St John the Baptist, and for the same reason: calling an adulterous king to repentance. The populace spotted the parallels, and the king was anxious that Fisher should not still be alive on the feast of St John the Baptist, 24th June. Therefore he was beheaded on Tower Hill on 22nd June (then the feast of St Alban, first martyr of Britain), and the similarity of his death with that of the Baptist was clearly seen by all.

St John Fisher went to his death with great dignity and faith. His body was stripped by the King's orders and then thrown naked into a rough grave. Later on his head was impaled on a pole on London Bridge, but its lifelike appearance made such an impression on Londoners that it was removed and thrown into the Thames, being replaced with that of St Thomas More, who had the same fate as John Fisher on 6th July. The surviving relics of St John Fisher are preserved at Stonyhurst College, Lancashire.

Blessed Mathew Flathers

Born at Weston, Yorkshire
Martyred at York, 21st March, 1607 under James I
Beatified on 22nd November, 1987
by Pope St John Paul II

Mathew Flathers was educated at Douai and ordained at Arras on 25th March 1606. Three months later he was sent to the English mission, but was discovered almost immediately by the agents of the Government; after the

Gunpowder Plot, the English state was particularly active in hunting down Catholic priests.

Flathers was brought to trial, under the statute of 27 Elizabeth, on the charge of receiving orders abroad, and condemned to death. By an act of clemency, this sentence was commuted to banishment for life; but after a brief exile, he returned to England and his mission. After ministering for a short time to Catholics in Yorkshire, he was again apprehended.

Brought to trial at York on the charge of being ordained abroad and exercising priestly functions in England, Flathers was offered his life on condition that he take the recently-enacted Oath of Allegiance. On his refusal, he was condemned to death and taken to the common place of execution outside Micklegate Bar, York, where he was hanged, drawn, and quartered in a particularly brutal manner.

Blessed William Freeman

Born at Manthorp, Yorkshire
Martyred at Warwick, 13th August, 1595
under Elizabeth I
Beatified on 15th December, 1929 by Pope Pius XI

William Freeman's parents were recusant Catholics, but he was conforming Anglican for some time. He was educated at Magdalen College, Oxford, and took his BA in 1581. He then lived for some years in London. He witnessed the execution of Edward Stransham in 1586. Strongly impressed with this example, he left England and was ordained priest in 1587 at Rheims.

Returning to England in 1589, Freeman worked for six years on the borders of Warwickshire. In January, 1595, a special commission was sent down to Stratford-on-Avon to search the house of Mrs Heaths, who had engaged Freeman's services as tutor to her son. William Freeman was arrested, and spent seven months in prison. He denied his priesthood, but also refused all offers to escape. Owing to the treachery of a fellow-prisoner, William Gregory, he was at last sentenced as a seminary priest and in spite of a protest of loyalty, suffered the death of a traitor at Warwick. On hearing his sentence of hanging, drawing and quartering, Blessed William sang the Te Deum. As he approached his place of execution he carried a crucifix, and protested aloud that if he had many lives, he would willingly lay them down for the sake of Him who had been pleased to die upon a cross for his redemption. Freeman asked the sheriff if he might be executed first, before the common criminals who were to die upon that day, but this was refused in the hope that seeing their deaths might terrify him into renouncing the Catholic faith in exchange for his life. On the contrary, this sight only made William Freeman more ardent in his desire to die for Christ.

John Fulthering

Born in Yorkshire
Martyred at York, 1st August, 1605 under James I

A zealous Catholic layman, John Fulthering worked with the Blessed Thomas Welbourne to persuade others to convert. He was executed at York alongside his fellow apostle on 1st August 1605.

Blessed Edward Fulthrop

Born in Yorkshire
Martyred at York, 4th July, 1597 under Elizabeth I
Beatified on 15th December, 1929 by Pope Pius XI

Blessed Edward Fulthrop was a Yorkshire gentleman, who was converted to the Catholic faith by the priest Blessed William Andleby, and for this was condemned to die the death of a traitor with him in York on 4th July 1597.

Blessed William Gibson

Born in Fife, Scotland, 1548
Martyred at York, 24th November, 1596
under Elizabeth I
Beatified on 22nd November, 1987
by Pope St John Paul II

Blessed William Gibson was the son of Lord Gibson of Goldingstones, Fife, Scotland, a judge of the High Court of Scotland, who was a "free baron" under charter of King James IV of Scotland. His great-uncle and namesake, Bishop William Gibson, Dean of Restalrig, had been one of the leading prelates in Scotland prior to the Scottish Reformation. He frequently represented King James V to the Holy See, and, with the support of Cardinal Beaton, his writings in defence of the Catholic faith had earned him the papal title of "Guardian of the Scottish Church".

The younger William Gibson ended up in Ripon, and was accused of treason for being a Catholic and denounced to the authorities. He was at once seized and committed to the custody of a noted pursuivant named Colyer, who treated him with indignity and severity. Gibson was sent in August 1593 to York Castle, where he was joined shortly thereafter by fellow future martyrs William Knight and George Errington, both arrested for participation in a rising.

A certain Anglican clergyman chanced to be among their fellow prisoners. To gain his freedom he had recourse to an act of treachery: feigning a desire to become a Roman Catholic, he won the confidence of Gibson and his two companions, who explained their faith to him. With the connivance of the authorities, he was directed to Henry Abbot, then at liberty, who endeavoured to procure a priest to reconcile him to the Church. When the clergyman had sufficient evidence, Gibson was arrested and, together with Knight and his two comrades, accused of attempting to persuade the clergyman to embrace Catholicism — an act of treason under the English Penal Laws. They were all found guilty, before (with the exception of Abbot, who was executed later) suffering hanging, drawing and quartering at York on 29th November 1596.

Blessed Ralph Grimston

Born at Nidd, Yorkshire
Martyred at York, 15th June, 1598 under Elizabeth I
Beatified on 22nd November, 1987
by Pope St John Paul II

Ralph Grimston was a Yorkshire gentleman, who assisted the priest Blessed Peter Snow in his missionary labours. For this, he was apprehended in the priest's company in May 1598 and convicted of felony for harbouring a seminary priest and accused of lifting his weapon to defend his companion and to prevent his arrest when they were taken. He was executed at York along with Peter Snow on 14th June 1598.

Blessed Robert Hardesty

Born in Yorkshire
Martyred at York, 24th September, 1589
under Elizabeth I
Beatified on 22nd November, 1987
by Pope St John Paul II

Robert Hardesty was a layman of great probity and piety who gave shelter to the priest Blessed William Spenser and in consequence suffered martyrdom with him.

Blessed William Harrington

Born at Mount St John, Yorkshire
Martyred at Tyburn, London, 18th February, 1594
under Elizabeth I
Beatified on 15th December, 1929 by Pope Pius XI

William Harrington's father had entertained Edmund Campion at the ancestral home, Mount St John, early in 1581. Young William, inspired by Campion, went abroad to train as a priest.

He was first at the seminary at Rheims, then went to study under the Jesuits at Tournai. He would have joined the order, but his health broke down and forced him to keep at home for the next six years.

In February 1591, however, he was able to return once more to Rheims, and, having been ordained, returned at midsummer 1592. The following May he fell into the hands of the English authorities, whereupon he was arrested and confined to the dungeons for several months. He was sentenced to be hanged, drawn and quartered at Tyburn for the crime of being a Catholic priest. William Harrington was given the chance to spare his life if he renounced the Catholic faith and attend Protestant services just once. William refused. He was tortured on the rack, hanged until not quite dead, then disembowelled, before being beheaded.

William's fate had an important literary side-effect. One of those who had sheltered him was Henry Donne, the brother of the poet John Donne. Henry was arrested, and died of the plague in Newgate Prison. John Donne was a Catholic too, but later embraced the Protestant Church of England, in an effort to spare his own life.

Venerable James Harrison

Born in the diocese of Litchfield
Martyred at York, 22nd March, 1602 under Elizabeth I
Declared Venerable in 1886 by Pope Leo XIII

Also known as Matthew, James Harrison was ordained at Rheims in 1583 and was sent on the English mission the following year. He fell into the hands of the persecutors just before the Lent assizes, 1601-2, and was sentenced to die for high treason on account of having been ordained priest abroad. When he was told by the keeper unexpectedly that he was to die the next day, Harrison showed not the slightest sign of trouble, but sat down to supper with a cheerful countenance, saying, "Let us eat and drink, for tomorrow we shall die." He drank the same cup as his Master the next day with great constancy and fervour.

Harrison's head was obtained and venerated by the English Franciscans at Douai.

Blessed William Hart

Born at Wells, 1558
Martyred at York, 15th March, 1583 under Elizabeth I
Beatified on 29th December, 1886 by Pope Leo XIII

William Hart was a scholar of Lincoln College, Oxford, but having taken his BA went to Douai in 1574, together with the Rector of Lincoln, John Bridgewater, a Yorkshireman, who took several of his students with him after announcing that he preferred the "old form of religion" to the novelties of "Calvinopapists and Puritans".

Hart moved with the English College to Rheims. He underwent a severe operation at Namur in 1578 and in 1579 went to Rome, where he took the English College oath and was ordained priest. He came back to England in 1581 and ministered in Yorkshire, particularly to Catholic prisoners. Hence he was present at the Mass in York Castle when Blessed William Lacy was captured, but escaped by standing up to his chin in the castle moat.

On Christmas Day 1582 Fr Hart was betrayed by an apostate in the house of St Margaret Clitherow, arrested, put in an underground dungeon, clapped in double irons, and then examined by the Dean of York and the Council of the North. At the Lent assizes he was tried for bringing papal writings into the country, going abroad without permission and reconciling people with the Church. William Hart was condemned to death by hanging, drawing and quartering.

He himself said, "The joy of this life is nothing, but the joy of the after life is everlasting."

Blessed John Hewitt

Born at York
Martyred at Mile End Green, London, 6th October, 1588 under Elizabeth I
Beatified on 15th December, 1929 by Pope Pius XI

The son of a York draper, John Hewitt was an undergraduate at Gonville and Caius College, Cambridge. He was one of four martyrs from that College, of whom Blessed William Dean and Blessed John Finglow were also Yorkshiremen.

Hewitt was ordained priest at Rheims in November 1585. He came to England, using the names Weldon and Savell as aliases, and was captured early in 1587, when he was exiled to the Netherlands. There he fell into the hands of the brutal Earl of Leicester, who arrested him and sent him back to England for trial.

Blessed John was charged with being ordained priest and entering England to exercise that ministry. He was led through the streets of London to Mile End, where he held two disputes with Protestant preachers before being hanged, drawn and quartered.

Blessed Richard Hill

Born in Yorkshire
Martyred at Durham, 27th May, 1590
under Elizabeth I
Beatified on 22nd November, 1987
by Pope St John Paul II

Richard Hill is one of the Dryburne Martyrs, three of whom were born in Yorkshire and one, (Blessed Edmund Duke) in Kent. They all arrived in the mid-1580s at the English College at Rheims to study for the priesthood.

Hill arrived at Rheims on 15th May 1587 and was ordained priest on 23rd September 1589 at Laon by Bishop Valentine Douglas, O.S.B.

Hill, Holiday, Hogg and Duke were all sent on the English mission on 22nd March 1590 but aroused suspicion by keeping together as a band and were arrested in County Durham soon after landing in the North of England. Given the 1585 Act making it a capital offence to be a Catholic priest in England the sentence of hanging, drawing and quartering was inevitable. The trial was at Durham and the sentence was carried out there. According to legend, "After the execution, it was noticed that a small stream near the site had completely dried up, and so the area is known as 'Dryburn' to this day."

With the priests were executed four common criminals, who declared that they too died Catholics. In the crowd were a good number of Catholics and reportedly when the priests' heads were as customary cut off and held up, only the officers and a Protestant minister or two would say "God save the Queen". It is also said that two Protestant spectators, Robert Maire and his wife Grace Maire, were converted to the Catholic faith.

Unusually the record of the event has survived in the registers of St Oswald's parish, Durham.

Blessed John Hogg

Born in Yorkshire
Martyred at Durham, 27th May, 1590 under Elizabeth I
Beatified on 22nd November, 1987
by Pope St John Paul II

Like Richard Hill and John Holiday, John Hogg was martyred in County Durham – one of the 'Dryburne Martyrs'.

Hill arrived at Rheims on 15th October 1587 and was ordained priest on 23rd September 1589 at Laon by Bishop Valentine Douglas, O.S.B.

Hill, Holiday, Hogg and Duke were all sent on the English mission on 22nd March 1590 but aroused suspicion by keeping together as a band and were arrested in County Durham soon after landing in the North of England. Given the 1585 Act making it a capital offence to be a Catholic priest in England, the sentence of hanging, drawing and quartering was inevitable. The trial was at Durham and the sentence was carried out there. According to legend, "After the execution, it was noticed that a small stream near the site had completely dried up, and so the area is known as 'Dryburn' to this day."

With the priests were executed four common criminals, who declared that they too died Catholics. In the crowd were a good number of Catholics and reportedly when the priests' heads were as customary cut off and held up, only the officers and a Protestant minister or two would say "God save the Queen". It is also said that two Protestant spectators, Robert Maire and his wife Grace Maire, were converted to the Catholic faith.

Blessed John Holiday

Born in Yorkshire
Martyred at Durham, 27th May, 1590 under Elizabeth I
Beatified on 22nd November, 1987
by Pope St John Paul II

John Holiday is the third Yorkshireman among the 'Dryburne Martyrs'.

Hill arrived at Rheims on 6th September 1584 and was ordained priest on 23rd September 1589 at Laon by Bishop Valentine Douglas, O.S.B.

On coming to England, he was arrested along with his fellow-priests Edmund Duke, Richard Hill, and John Hogg, put on trial in Durham, and there made to suffer the death of a traitor, simply for his priesthood.

Venerable Richard Horner

Born at Bolton-Bridge, Yorkshire,
Martyred at York, 4th September, 1598 under Elizabeth I
Declared Venerable in 1886 by Pope Leo XIII

Educated at Douai, Richard Horner was ordained priest in 1595 and was in the same year sent on the English mission. He fell into the hands of the enemies of the Faith and was arraigned and condemned merely as a Catholic priest. He suffered much in prison and was executed in York for high treason.

Eleanor Hunt

Died in York Castle, 1600 under Elizabeth I

Eleanor Hunt was a widow, who gave shelter to the priest, Blessed Christopher Wharton, in her home in York. She was arrested with him and confined in York Castle. Put on trial felony, she was condemned, and refused life and liberty in exchange for conformity to the state religion. Mrs Hunt died in prison before any sentence could be carried out.

Blessed Thurstan Hunt

Born at Carlton Hall, near Leeds, Yorkshire
Martyred in Lancashire, March 1601 under Elizabeth I
Beatified on 22nd November, 1987
by Pope St John Paul II

Thurstan Hunt was a gentleman by birth and was educated at Douai, where he was ordained priest in April 1584. The following year he set off on the English mission and worked mainly in Lancashire. He and others attempted to rescue a priest who was being carried off to prison – Blessed Robert Middleton, Margaret Clitherow's nephew. In consequence of this brave endeavour, Hunt was himself arrested, recognized as a priest, and executed for high treason.

Blessed Francis Ingleby

Born at Ripley Castle, Yorkshire, c.1551
Martyred at York, 3rd June, 1586 under Elizabeth I
Beatified on 22nd November, 1987
by Pope St John Paul II

Francis Ingleby was the fourth son of Sir William Ingleby of Ripley Castle and his wife Mary. Another of their sons, David, was also a staunch Catholic, who fled abroad. Francis is thought to have been a scholar of Brasenose College, Oxford and then a student of the Inner Temple. He arrived on 18th August 1582 at the English College, Rheims, where he lived at his own expense, being ordained priest on Christmas Eve 1583. We have a description of Ingleby's appearance: "short but well-made, fair-complexioned, with a chestnut beard, and a slight cast in his eyes."

Blessed Francis returned to England and set about the mission in York with great enthusiasm. Dressed as a poor man, suspicion was aroused when one of his companions showed him more deference than would be usual for someone in such an apparently humble station. When St Margaret Clitherow was tried, Francis Ingleby was one of the priests she was charged with harbouring. He himself was condemned under the 'Jesuits etc' Act of 1584 and sentenced to be hanged, drawn and quartered at the Knavesmire in York. When sentence was pronounced, Ingelby spoke these words from Psalm 26: "Credo videre bona Domini in terra viventium" – I believe to see the good things of the Lord in the land of the living.

As the shackles were fastened onto Ingelby's legs at the prison door he smiled and said, "I fear me I shall be overproud of my boots."

Saint Luke Kirby

Born at Bedale, Yorkshire, c.1549
Martyred at Tyburn, London, 30th May, 1582 under Elizabeth I
Beatified on 29th December, 1886 by Pope Leo XIII
Canonized on 25th October, 1970 by Pope St Paul VI

Luke Kirby probably studied at Cambridge before converting to the faith at Louvain and entering Douai College in 1576. He was ordained priest at Cambrai in 1577 and spent just over two months on the English mission in 1578. He then went to Rome, and took the college oath at the English College on St George's Day 1579. During his time in Rome, Kirby was known for practising charity towards his countrymen, Catholic or not, who needed help. Although not rich himself, he was generous with money and his energy.

In 1580 Luke Kirby was chosen to accompany SS Edmund Campion and Ralph Sherwin to England. They left Rome on 14th April and arrived at Rheims on 31st May. Together with William Hartley, Kirby went along the French coast on foot, and landed at Dover in June, where he was immediately arrested. At first he was placed in the Gatehouse, Westminster, before being transferred to the Tower on 4th December, where he was subjected to the horrific torture known as the 'Scavenger's Daughter' for more than an hour on 9th December.

By November 1581 St Edmund Campion had also been captured, and the two were put on trial together, charged with High Treason simply on the grounds of their being Catholic priests. They were inevitably found guilty, but St Luke had to wait until May 1582 to be hanged, drawn and quartered at Tyburn. He declared that he was guilty of no treason, declared that he died solely for the Catholic faith, and resisted the attempts of Protestant officials to trick him into denying the truths of the Catholic religion. Finally they tried to persuade him to pray with them, which he refused, since they were not of the same faith, and instead he recited the Our Father in Latin, before being cruelly butchered.

St Luke Kirby's ministry in England lasted so short a time, yet he stands as a bold witness to the eternal truths of the faith, and to the value of the priesthood.

Blessed Richard Kirkman

Born at Addington, Yorkshire
Martyred at York, 22nd August, 1582 under Elizabeth I
Beatified on 29th December, 1886 by Pope Leo XIII

Blessed Richard Kirkman was ordained priest at the English College, Rheims on Holy Saturday 1579 and then left for England on 3rd August that year, with St Alexander Briant and three others. Kirkman found a home with Robert Dymoke, hereditary champion of England, at Scrivelsby Hall in Lincolnshire. Fr Kirkman was able to pass himself as the tutor to Dymoke's sons, until Robert Dymoke was himself arrested for recusancy in September 1580. (Dymoke was to die in Lincoln Gaol as a confessor for the faith). At this point Richard Kirkman fled north but was arrested near Wakefield on 8th August 1582. The Lord President of the North, who encouraged the harrying of Catholics, was the Earl of Huntington, a fanatical and ferocious Puritan.

Blessed Richard was imprisoned together with Blessed William Lacy in York Castle, and hanged, drawn and quartered at the same time on 22nd August. Richard Kirkham's last words are said to have been from Psalm 119: "'Woe to me that I dwell in Meshech, that I live among the tents of Kedar! Too long have I lived among those who hate peace."

Blessed William Knight

Born at South Duffield, Yorkshire, 1572
Martyred at York, 29th November, 1596
under Elizabeth I
Beatified on 22nd November, 1987
by Pope St John Paul II

Blessed William Knight, a secret convert to the Catholic Church, was the son of Leonard Knight and lived at South Duffield, a hamlet currently in the Selby District of North Yorkshire. On coming of age, Knight claimed from his uncle some property which had been left to him by his father. The uncle denounced him to the authorities for being a Catholic. He was at once seized and committed to the custody of a pursuivant named Colyer, who treated him with indignity and severity.

Knight was sent in October, 1593, to York Castle, where William Gibson and George Errington were already confined, the latter having been arrested some years before for participation in a rising in the North.

A Church of England clergyman was among the prisoners at York. To gain his freedom, he had recourse to an act of treachery: feigning a desire to convert to the Roman Church, he won the confidence of Knight and his two companions, who explained their faith to him. With the connivance of the authorities, he was directed to Henry Abbot, then at liberty, who endeavoured to procure a priest to reconcile him to the Church. When the minister had sufficient evidence, Abbot was arrested and, together with Knight and his two comrades, accused of attempting to persuade the clergyman to embrace Roman Catholicism — an act of treason under the penal laws.

The men were found guilty, and, with the exception of Abbot, who was executed later, suffered hanging, drawing and quartering at York on 29th November 1596. Knight was about 24 years old when he died.

Blessed William Lacy

Born at 'Hanton', Yorkshire
(probably either Houghton or Tosside)
Martyred at York, 22nd August, 1582 under Elizabeth I
Beatified on 29th December, 1886 by Pope Leo XIII

Blessed William Lacy was married twice, and two of his stepsons became Jesuits. As a layman he held a position under the Crown (perhaps as a coroner) and already suffered for the faith, paying many fines, being deprived of his livelihood and finally imprisoned for a time at Hull. After the death of his second wife he went to Rome, where he was ordained priest, before returning to England, passing by the Holy House at Loreto on his way.

In 1582 Fr Lacy was arrested following a Mass said by Thomas Bell at York Castle. He was cruelly treated, loaded with heavy irons, confined in an underground dungeon and then hanged, drawn and quartered along with Blessed Richard Kirkman on 22nd August.

Blessed Richard Langley

Born at Grimthorpe, Yorkshire
Martyred at York, 1st December 1586
under Elizabeth I
Beatified on 15th December, 1929 by Pope Pius XI

Richard Langley was probably born at Grimthorpe in Yorkshire. From his father, Richard Langley, of Rathorpe Hall, Walton, he probably inherited Rathorpe, but for the greater part of his life continued to reside on his estate at Ousethorpe, in the East Riding of Yorkshire. His mother was Joan Beaumont of Mirfield. He married Agnes, daughter of Richard Hansby, New Malton, by whom he had one son, Christopher (b. 1565), and four daughters.

During the Elizabethan period Langley assisted the Catholic clergy; his house was offered as an asylum to priests. He constructed a subterranean retreat, perhaps beneath the Grimthorpe dwelling, which afforded them sanctuary. This refuge was betrayed to the President of the North, and on 28th October 1586, a strong band of military was despatched, several justices and Anglican ministers joining them, to make a visitation of the Grimthorpe and Ousethorpe houses. Two priests were found in hiding at the former; at the latter Langley himself was seized. All three were carried to York, committed to prison, and subsequently arraigned before the President of the North, the priests because of their office and Langley for harbouring them.

During the investigation Langley would not take the oath of the Queen's ecclesiastical supremacy, nor ingratiate himself with the Lord President or Privy Council. The first jury was discharged and replaced by another. Langley was condemned to death, without any evidence being adduced to establish the fact that he had knowingly sheltered seminary priests; and he was hanged at York. His remains were refused an honourable burial.

Blessed Joseph Lambton

Born at Malton-in-Rydake, Yorkshire
Martyred at Newcastle, 24th July, 1592 under Elizabeth I
Beatified on 22nd November, 1987
by Pope St John Paul II

Joseph Lambton was the second son of Thomas Lambton of Malton-in-Rydale, Yorkshire, and Katharine, daughter of Robert Birkhead of West Brandon, Durham. Joseph's maternal uncle, George Birkhead was Archpriest in England from 1608 to 1614. In September 1584 Thomas was admitted to the English College, then at Rheims, along with Anthony Page and two others. It was while he was at Rheims, that Parliament passed legislation by which priests and religious entering the realm were to be deemed traitors unless within three days of their arrival they had taken the Oath of Supremacy before a Justice of the Peace.

In August 1589 he went to the English College, Rome. Eager to go on the English mission, he was allowed to curtail his theological course, and was ordained priest in the Lateran

Basilica on the 28th March 1592, with a dispensation as Lambton was two months short of the canonical age. He left for England to work in Westmorland on 22 April 1592. He was arrested at Newcastle soon after landing and condemned with Edward Waterson at the next assizes.

In order to avoid a crowd, the execution was scheduled for early Monday rather than the previous Saturday. It was decided that Lambton should be executed alone, and Waterson given a brief reprieve to allow him time to consider changing his views. Lambton was cut down alive, and the hangman refused to complete the sentence, which was carried out by a Frenchman practising as a surgeon at Kenton. The sheriff then took part of the remains and showed them to Waterson in an effort to frighten him, but Waterson viewed them as holy relics.

Blessed John Lockwood

Born at Sowerby, Yorkshire, c.1555
Martyred at York, 13th April, 1642 under Charles I
Beatified on 15th December, 1929 by Pope Pius XI

John Lockwood was the eldest son of Christopher Lockwood of Sowerby, Yorkshire, by Clare, eldest daughter of Christopher Lascelles, of Sowerby and Brackenborough Castle, Yorkshire. With his brother Francis he arrived at Rheims in November 1579.

Francis was ordained in 1587, but John entered the English College, Rome, in October 1595, and was ordained priest on 26th January 1597. He was sent on the English mission, in April 1598.

After suffering imprisonment Lockwood was banished in 1610, but returned, and was again taken and condemned to death, but reprieved. He was finally captured at Wood End, Gatenby, the residence of Bridget Gatenby, and executed with Edmund Catherick. Extraordinarily, this priest was eighty-seven years old when he was killed. To Cuthbert Langdale, the priest-hunter who had apprehended him, Lockwood gave five shillings, for the trouble that it took conveying such an old man to York Castle, and the two parted as friends.

At the time of the execution of Edmund Catherick and John Lockwood, King Charles I and the Prince of Wales (later King Charles II) were in residence at the King's Manor. The two martyrs were dragged through the streets of York on a hurdle. Mr Catherick took fright when it came to climb the ladder to the scaffold, and so John Lockwood undertook to ascend first, saying, "O let us run in spirit to our Saviour in the garden, and call upon Him in His agony and bloody sweat." Lockwood's age made it difficult to climb, and he had to be assisted by two men, to whom he gave a shilling each. After a few minutes in silent prayer Blessed John Lockwood's last words were, "Jesus, my Saviour! Jesus, my Redeemer, receive my soul! Jesus, be to me a Jesus!" The executioner at first refused to cut up the bodies of the two martyrs, saying that he would rather hang himself than cover his hands in innocent blood. Urged on by a wicked woman, he hacked them to pieces however, and Mr Lockwood's head was impaled on top of Bootham Bar, where the King could not come out of his house without seeing the bloodied relic of this old Eleazar.

Blessed Anthony Middleton

Born at Middleton-Tyas, Yorkshire
Martyred at Clerkenwell, London, 6th May, 1590
under Elizabeth I
Beatified on 15th December, 1929 by Pope Pius XI

Blessed Anthony Middleton was the son of Ambrose Middleton of Barnard Castle, Durham, and Cecile, daughter of Anthony Crackenthorpe of Howgill Castle, Westmoreland. He entered the English College at Rheims in January 1582; was ordained on 30th May 1586, and went to England in the same year. His work lay in London and the neighbourhood and he laboured very successfully. Being "low of stature and of a young look" for a long time he was not suspected of being a priest. However he was captured at a house in Clerkenwell by priest-catchers pretending to be Catholics.

On the ladder Blessed Anthony said: "I call God to witness I die merely for the Catholic Faith, and for being a priest of the true Religion"; and someone present called out, "Sir, you have spoken very well". The martyr was cut down and disembowelled while yet alive.

Blessed Robert Middleton

Born at York
Martyred in Lancashire, March, 1601 under Elizabeth I
Beatified on 22nd November, 1987
by Pope St John Paul II

Blessed Robert Middleton was the nephew of St Margaret Clitherow and worked as a priest on the English mission. He was captured along with the priest Blessed Thurstan Hunt in London and another priest. They were sent to Lancashire for trial and found guilty of high treason, for which all three suffered hanging, drawing and quartering.

Blessed Robert Morton

Born at Bawtry, Yorkshire, c.1548
Martyred at Lincoln's Inn Fields, London, 28th August, 1588 under Elizabeth I
Beatified on 15th December, 1929 by Pope Pius XI

Robert Morton was ordained deacon in Rome and priest at Rheims in 1587. He was condemned at Newgate merely for his priesthood, and hanged, drawn and quartered alongside the layman Blessed Hugh Moor, who had been reconciled to the Church. 28th August 1588 was the day of seven Catholic martyrdoms in London, as a result of the hysteria following the Armada.

Blessed John Nelson

Born at Skelton, York, c.1535
Martyred at Tyburn, London, 3rd February, 1578 under Elizabeth I
Beatified on 29th December, 1886 by Pope Leo XIII

John Nelson was the son of Sir Nicholas Nelson and went to Douai to train as a priest when he was nearly forty. Two of his four brothers, Martin and Thomas, would later follow him there to become priests. He was ordained in June 1576. In November 1576 Nelson left for England, probably ministering in London.

He was arrested on 1st December 1578 at home, "late in the evening as he was saying the Nocturne of the Matins for the next day following", and was put into Newgate Prison as a suspected Papist. When interrogated about a week later, he refused to take the oath recognizing the Queen's supremacy in spiritual matters, and was induced by the commissioners to declare the Queen a schismatic. Under the Legislation of 1571, this was high treason and was punishable by death. He was condemned to death on 1st February 1578, and was confined after the trial in an underground dungeon in the Tower of London, the Pit of the Tower. While in prison he subsisted on bread and water but was able to say Mass. Nelson wrote to the French Jesuits, seeking admission to the Society, which they were happy to grant.

On his execution day Fr Nelson refused to see several Protestant ministers, after meeting with family members. He was taken to Tyburn and was allowed to speak before the bystanders, who were mostly hostile. When asked to beg pardon of the Queen, he responded, "I will ask no pardon of her, for I have never offended her." He then asked any Catholics in the crowd to pray with him as he recited the Creed, our Father and Hail Mary, in Latin. He was hanged and cut down alive, then quartered. His last words were, reportedly, "I forgive the Queen and all the authors of my death". Blessed John Nelson's head was displayed on London Bridge, and portions of his body on each of the four city gates.

Blessed Edward Osbaldeston

Born at Osbaldeston Hall, near Blackburn, Lancashire, c.1560
Martyred at York, 16th November, 1594
under Elizabeth I
Beatified on 22nd November, 1987
by Pope St John Paul II

Edward Osbaldeston was the son of Thomas Osbaldeston, and nephew of Edward Osbaldeston, of Osbaldeston Hall. He went to the English College of Douai, then at Rheims, where he was ordained deacon in December, 1583, and priest on 21st September 1585. He was sent on the English mission in April 1589, and was apprehended at night through the instrumentality of an apostate priest named Thomas Clark at an inn at Tollerton, Yorkshire, upon St. Jerome's day, 30th September 1594. Osbaldeston had said his first Mass on the feast day of St. Jerome, and in consequence had a great devotion to that saint.

The day following his arrest Osbaldeston was taken to York where he was tried at the next assizes and attained of high treason for being a priest. Bishop Challoner prints the greater part of a letter addressed by the martyr to his fellow-prisoners in York Castle, the full text of which is still extant, and which reveals the great humility and serene trust in God with which he anticipated his death.

Blessed Edward Oldcorne

Born at York, 1561
Martyred at Red Hill, Worcester, 7th April, 1606
under James I
Beatified on 15th December, 1929 by Pope Pius XI

Edward Oldcorne was the son of John Oldcorne, a York bricklayer, and his wife Mary. John was a Protestant, but Mary was a Catholic, who had spent time in prison for her faith. Edward was educated at St Peter's School, and his classmates included John and Christopher Wright and Guy Fawkes, all three of whom were later implicated in the 'Gunpowder Plot'. Edward at first became a doctor, but then went to the English College at Rheims, and afterwards to Rome, where he was ordained priest in 1587 and entered the Society of Jesus in 1588.

Later that same year, Blessed Edward returned to England with Fr John Gerard, and he worked with Fr Henry Garnet from 1589 in Warwickshire and Worcestershire. Oldcorne's name is associated with some of the most famous recusant houses such as Coughton Court, and Hindlip Hall near Baddlesley Clinton. Both of these had priest hiding-holes constructed by St Nicholas Owen to help Catholic priests avoid capture.

Although we know little about Fr Oldcorne's work during these years, it is evident that he made converts and was able to celebrate Mass around the West Midlands for quite some time. In 1601 he went to St Winefride's Well in North Wales to seek a cure for throat cancer. His prayers were answered, and so four years later he took a pilgrimage of some thirty people to give thanks. The pilgrims included some of the heroes of hidden Catholic England: Fathers Oswald Tesimond, Ralph Ashley, Henry Garnet and John Gerard, together with the layman Everard Digby and his wife.

Once the Gunpowder plot was discovered, Oldcorne came under suspicion because of his association with the plotters. He hid at Hindlip, along with Nicholas Owen, Henry Garnet and Ralph Ashley. That eight days of searching failed to uncover them is a testament to the ingenuity of Nicholas Owen's hiding places. The searchers, led by Sir Henry Bromley, would have given up by then had not one of the plotters, Humphrey Littleton, told them that Oldcorne and Garnet were hiding at Hindlip. After eight days the conditions in the hiding places became unbearable, and the brave Jesuits gave themselves up. (Littleton later asked forgiveness for his betrayal.)

At his trial no evidence could be produced linking Fr Oldcorne to the plot, but he was nevertheless convicted. He was hanged, drawn and quartered at Red Hill, Worcester with three others. One, Ralph Ashley, kissed Oldcorne's feet as he ascended the ladder and said, "What a happy man am I to follow in the steps of my sweet father." Blessed Edward died invoking St Winefride.

When the executioner decapitated Oldcorne, the blow was so forceful that one of his eyes flew out of its socket. While his body was being parboiled, a Catholic sympathizer retrieved the eye, which, together with the rope that hanged him, is preserved at Stonyhurst.

Blessed Anthony Page

Born at Harrow-on-the-Hill, Middlesex, 1563
Martyred at York, 30th April, 1593 under Elizabeth I
Beatified on 22nd November, 1987
by Pope St John Paul II

Anthony Page was of gentle birth and matriculated at Christ Church, Oxford on 23rd November 1581. He entered the English College, Rheims on 30th September 1584 along with Joseph Lambton, and received minor orders in April 1585. He was ordained deacon at Laon on 22nd September 1590, and priest at Soissons on 21st September 1591. Anthony Champney, who was his contemporary at Rheims, in his manuscript history of the reign of Elizabeth I of England, as quoted by Richard Challoner, describes him as describes him "of more than common learning and piety, and as having endeared himself to all by his singular candour of mind and sweetness of behaviour."

On Candlemas 1593, there was a great search for priests ordered in the north, and he was found at Haworth Hall near York, in a hiding place at the bottom of a haystack. He was condemned for being a priest, and was hanged, drawn, and quartered at York on 30th April 1593.

Blessed Thomas Palasor

Born at Ellerton-on-Swale, Yorkshire
Martyred at Durham, 9th August, 1600 under Elizabeth I
Beatified on 22nd November, 1987
by Pope St John Paul II

Palasor arrived at Rheims on 24th July 1592, and set out for the English College, Valladolid on 24th August 1592. There, he was ordained priest in 1596.

He was arrested in the house of John Norton, of Ravenswroth, nearly Lamesley, County Durham. Norton seems to have been the second son of Richard Norton, of Norton Conyers, attainted for his share in the Rising of the North in 1569. Norton and his wife were arrested at the same time, with a noble English gentleman, the Blessed John Talbot, one of the Talbots of Thornton-le-Street, North Riding of Yorkshire.

All four were tried at Durham and condemned to death, Palasor for being a priest, and the others for assisting him. Another gentleman was condemned at the same time but saved his life by conforming to the Church of England, as the others might have done. Mrs Norton, being supposed to be with child, was reprieved. The others were executed together.

Richard Challoner tells how an attempt to poison Palasor and his companions made by the gaoler's wife resulted in the conversion of her maid-servant Mary Day.

Blessed Thomas Percy

Born 1528
Martyred at York, 22nd August, 1572 under Elizabeth I
Beatified on 13th May, 1895 by Pope Leo XIII

Thomas Percy was the eldest son of Sir Thomas Percy and the nephew of the Earl of Northumberland. When Thomas was eight years old, his father, Sir Thomas Percy, was executed, on 2nd June 1537, for having taken part in the Pilgrimage of Grace. Thomas and his brother Henry were taken away from their mother and entrusted to Sir Thomas Tempest.

During the happier period of Queen Mary I's reign, Thomas was knighted and regained his ancestral honours and lands. He become Member of Parliament for Westmorland in 1554 and was made governor of Prudhoe Castle. He besieged and took Scarborough Castle when it was seized by rebels. In 1557 he was created Earl of Northumberland, his uncle having died without issue twenty years before. As Warden General of the Marches, Percy fought and defeated the Scots.

Despite the earl's loyalty to the Catholic Church, Elizabeth Tudor continued to favour him, making him a Knight of the Garter in 1563. Percy was disturbed by rumours of Elizabeth's excommunication and the unrest of Catholic gentry in the north and wrote to the Pope asking for advice.

After the failure of the 1569 Rising of the North, Thomas Percy fled to Scotland and became the prisoner of the nefarious Protestant, the Earl of Morton. This Scots nobleman sold Percy to the English for two thousand pounds three years later, and the Earl of Northumberland was conducted to York. There he was offered his life in exchange for renouncing his Catholic faith, which he refused. Thomas Percy was beheaded publicly, and his headless body buried at St Crux Church.

Blessed John Pibush

Born at Thirsk, Yorkshire
Martyred at Camberwell, 18th February, 1601
under Elizabeth I
Beatified on 15th December, 1929 by Pope Pius XI

    John Pibush was probably a son of Thomas Pibush, of Great Fencote, and Jane, sister to Peter Danby of Scotton. He came to Rheims on 4th August 1580, received minor orders and subdiaconate in September, and diaconate in December, 1586, and was ordained priest on 14th March 1587.

    Pibush was sent on the English mission in January 1588-9, arrested at Moreton-in-Marsh, Gloucestershire, in 1593, and sent to London, where he arrived before 24th July. The Privy Council committed him to the Gatehouse at Westminster, where he remained a year. He was then tried at the Gloucester Assizes for being a priest, but not sentenced, and was returned to Gloucester gaol, whence he escaped on 19th February (1594-5). The next day he was recaptured at Matson and taken back to Gloucester gaol, whence he was sent to the Marshalsea, London, and again tried at Westminster on 1st July 1595.

    Blessed John was sentenced to suffer the penalties of high treason at St. Thomas's Waterings, and in the meantime was to be returned to the Marshalsea. However, by the end of the year he was in the Queen's Bench prison, where he remained for more than five years. The sentence was carried out after one year's notice. After his death, John Pibush's lungs were found to have been so much damaged by his stay in prison, that he would have died soon in any case. Nevertheless, he had managed to celebrate clandestine Masses in prison and to be of great spiritual benefit to the other prisoners.

John Pickering

Martyred at Tyburn, London, 25th May, 1537
under Henry VIII

John Pickering, O.P., was a Dominican friar and the Prior of York Blackfriars. This Dominican Friary was founded at the Chapel of St Mary Magdalene in the South-West corner of York in 1227. The friars were probably temporarily housed at Goodramgate before that date. The prior, John Pickering, was executed at Tyburn in 1537 for taking part in the Pilgrimage of Grace. The friary was surrendered in 1538.

Blessed Thomas Pormort

Born at Kingston-upon-Hull, Yorkshire, c.1559
Martyred at St Paul's Churchyard, London,
29th February, 1592 under Elizabeth I
Beatified on 22nd November, 1987
by Pope St John Paul II

After receiving some education at Cambridge, Thomas Pormort went to Rheims, and then Rome, where he was ordained priest in 1587. He entered the household of Owen Lewis, Bishop of Cassano.

In April 1590, Pormort became prefect of studies in the Swiss college at Milan. He was relieved of this office, and started for England, on 15th September, without waiting for his faculties. Crossing the St Gotthard Pass, he reached Brussels before 29th November. There he became manservant to Mrs. Geoffrey Pole, under the name of Whitgift, the Protestant archbishop Whitgift being his godfather. With her he went to Antwerp, intending to proceed to Flushing, and thence to England.

He was arrested in London on St. James's Day (25th July), 1591, but he managed to escape. In August or September, 1591, he was again taken, and committed to Bridewell, whence he was removed to Topcliffe's house. Topcliffe was the notorious priest-hunter. Pormort was repeatedly racked and sustained a rupture in consequence. On 8th February following he was convicted of high treason for being a seminary priest, and for reconciling John Barwys, or Burrows, haberdasher, to the Catholic Church. He pleaded that he had no faculties; but he was found guilty.

At the bar he accused Topcliffe of having boasted to him of indecent familiarities with the Queen. Hence Topcliffe obtained a mandamus to the sheriff to proceed with the execution, though Archbishop Whitgift endeavoured to delay it and make his godson conform, and though (it is said) Pormort would have admitted conference with Protestant ministers. The gibbet was erected over against the haberdasher's shop, and Pormort was kept standing two hours on the ladder, while Topcliffe vainly urged him to withdraw his accusation.

Blessed Nicholas Postgate

Born at Egton, Yorkshire, 1596
Martyred at York, 7th August, 1679 under Charles II
Beatified on 22nd November, 1987
by Pope St John Paul II

Nicholas Postgate was born at Kirkdale House, Egton, Yorkshire, England. He entered Douai College, in July 1621. And was ordained priest in 1628. He was sent to the mission on 29th June 1630, and worked in England for the Catholic religion, finally settling back to Ugthorpe, not far from his birthplace, in the 1660s. His parish, which was known by the extinct name of Blackamoor, extended between Guisborough, Pickering and Scarborough.

Although anti-Catholic feeling in England had subsided a good deal at that time, it flared up again due to the fake Popish Plot of 1678; this followed a false testimony from Titus Oates in which he claimed there was a conspiracy to instal a Catholic king, and he managed to ferment a renewed and fierce persecution of English Catholics. It was to be the last time that Catholics were put to death in England for their faith; one of the last victims - but not the very last - was Nicholas Postgate.

During the panic engineered by Oates, a prominent Protestant magistrate in London, Sir Edmund Berry Godfrey, was murdered and Oates loudly blamed the Catholics; Sir Edmund's manservant, John Reeves, set out to get his revenge. For reasons which are not clear, he decided to base his actions in the Whitby area, possibly because he knew that priests arrived there from France.

Nicholas Postgate was apprehended by the exciseman Reeves, while carrying out a baptism at the house of Matthew Lyth at Little Beck, near Whitby. Reeves, with a colleague called William Cockerill, raided the house during the ceremony and caught the priest, then aged 82. Postgate was condemned for being a priest. He was hanged, disembowelled and quartered at York, His quarters were given to his friends and interred. One of the hands was sent to Douai College.

Reeves was listed in a treasury book as having been paid twenty-two shillings for his apprehension of Nicholas Postgate but some believe he did not receive the money before he committed suicide by drowning.

Nicholas Postgate's portable altar stone hangs at the front of the altar at Saint Joseph's Catholic Church, Pickering, where it is now venerated. Every year since 1974 an open-air service has been held – alternately in Egton Bridge and Ugthorpe – in honour of Nicholas Postgate. The pub in Egton Bridge is called 'The Postgate" in his honour.

Blessed Alexander Rawlins

Born at Oxford, 1560
Martyred at York, 7th April, 1595, under Elizabeth I
Beatified on 15th December, 1929 by Pope Pius XI

While Richard Challoner says that Rawlins was born somewhere on the border between Worcestershire and Gloucestershire, Rawlins himself stated to the examiners that he was born a Catholic in the city of Oxford. He went to school in Winchester before continuing his studies at Hart

Hall at Oxford. He then went to London, where he apprenticed himself to an apothecary.

In June 1586, he was arrested for the second time, with Swithun Wells, a known Catholic sympathizer, and seminarian Christopher Dryland and imprisoned in Newgate. After imprisonment, he was banished as "an obstinate Papist". Sailing from Southampton he landed at Saint-Malo and proceeded to Picardy. He travelled widely, mostly on foot, going to Rome, and Paris before arriving at Rheims, where he entered the college in December 1587. Rawlins was ordained a priest at Soissons on 18th March 1590 and sent on the English mission on 9th April. He arrived in England as a missioner with Edmund Gennings and Hugh Sewell. His mother's maiden name was Yeale, and Rawlins sometimes went by the alias "Francis Yeale".

Rawlins worked in York and Durham. On Christmas Day 1594 Rawlins was arrested at Winston, Durham. In the spring of 1595, he was in York awaiting trial, where he was joined by Henry Walpole. On Monday 7th April they were both hanged, drawn and quartered at Knavesmire. Rawlins was put to death first. The hangmen would have cut him down to be disembowelled alive, but they were stayed by a gentleman on horseback who made them wait until Rawlins was dead, and then lower the rope so his body should not fall.

Blessed William Richardson

Born at Wales, Yorkshire,
Martyred at Tyburn, London, 17th February 1603 under Elizabeth I
Beatified on 15th December, 1929 by Pope Pius XI

William Richardson studied for the priesthood at seminaries in Valladolid and then Seville. He was ordained sometime between 1594 and 1600. William was then sent back to England, where he used the alias William Anderson. Soon after arriving in England, he was betrayed by a trusted person, arrested in Gray's Inn and imprisoned.

Richardson was tried and convicted within a week and hanged, drawn, and quartered. His was the final martyrdom to take place during the reign of Queen Elizabeth I, as she was to die herself the next month. As Bishop Challoner writes, "Five weeks after Mr. Richardson's death, the Queen herself was called to the bar, to take her trial, before the Great Judge."

Blessed John Robinson

Born at Fernsby, Yorkshire
Martyred at Ipswich, 1st October, 1588 under Elizabeth I
Beatified on 15th December, 1929 by Pope Pius XI

John Robinson lived for some time in the world in the married state, but on becoming a widower he went over to Rheims, was ordained, and sent on the Mission. He was a man of great simplicity and sincerity, and he used to say that, "if he could not dispute for the faith as well as some of the others, he could die for it as well as the best."

Robinson was apprehended in the very port where he landed, and cast into the Clink prison. His fellow-prisoners, in respect to his age and probity, called him "Father," and he in return styled them his "bairns," and when they were sent off to be executed in different parts of the Kingdom, the good old man lamented for days exceedingly, until at last the warrant for his own execution arrived. To the bearer of the warrant he gave all his money, and on his knees gave God thanks.

He was sent to suffer at Ipswich, a long journey (82 miles) taken on foot, but he refused to put on boots, as he said, "These feet of mine have never worn them, and they can well travel now without them, for they will be well repaid."

Blessed John Rochester

Born at Terling, Essex, c.1498
Martyred at York, 11th May, 1537 under Henry VIII
Beatified on 29th December, 1886 by Pope Leo XIII

John Rochester was a monk of the London Charterhouse. In May 1535, three English Carthusians became the first martyrs of the English reformation when they were executed at Tyburn for refusing to agree to the royal supremacy over the Church. Three more monks of the London Charterhouse follwed in June – in the end fifteen members of that illustrious community were to be martyred. Fr Rochester was one of the monks who was taken to other Carthusian houses, in his case to the Charterhouse of St Michael in Hull.

After the Pilgrimage of Grace in October 1536, Dom John Rochester and Dom James Walworth were brought to York to stand trial for treason before the Duke of Norfolk, Lord President of the Council of the North. On 11th May 1537 the two monks became the first martyrs to suffer in York when they were publicly hanged, and their bodies then hung in chains from the city battlements.

Blessed Richard Simpson

Born at Well, Yorkshire, c.1553
Martyred at St Mary's Bridge, Derbyshire, 24th July, 1588 under Elizabeth I
Beatified on 22nd November, 1997
by Pope St John Paul II

Blessed Richard Simpson was an Anglican clergyman, but later converted to Catholicism He was imprisoned in York as a Catholic recusant; on being released, he went to Douai College, where he was admitted on 19th May 1577. The date of his ordination is unknown, but on 17th September 1577, Simpson set out for England to work as a missionary priest. He carried out his ministry in Lancashire and Derbyshire.

According to Challoner, Simpson was arrested and banished in 1585, but returned quickly to England. While travelling in the Peak District, in January 1588, he met a stranger who pretended so successfully to be a Catholic, that Simpson revealed his priesthood. The man denounced him at the next town, and he was arrested. He was imprisoned in Derby, and was condemned to death for treason at the Lenten Assizes. However, he was reprieved until the Summer Assizes.

Traditional accounts of Simpson's life state that the stay of execution was granted because he had given some indication that he would conform and attend an Anglican service, or hear a sermon. There is no record that he actually did so. According to Connelly, his surrender was not complete, and did not satisfy the judge, since he was not released but merely remanded for a second trial. Sweeney offers an alternative explanation for his reprieve. He points out that the execution of priests stopped for ten months in September 1587, the last one being that of George Douglas at York on 9th September. They were resumed ten months later, with the execution of Richard Simpson and his companions. Sweeney suggests that Elizabeth and her government, on hearing news of the preparations that Philip of Spain was making for his enterprise, may have decided to halt the persecution of Catholics in order to remove one of his complaints. By July 1588, the Armada was on its way, and there was no longer any motive for sparing priests. Simpson and his companions were the first of thirty-two priests martyred that year.

In Derby Gaol, before his second trial, Richard Simpson met with two other priests, Nicholas Garlick and Robert Ludlam. Traditional accounts indicate that they brought the wavering priest back to the Catholic Faith. Whether his reprieve was because of an agreement to attend a Protestant service or because of a temporary ban on executing priests, it is certain that at his second trial, on 23rd July, Simpson firmly declared himself a Catholic, and was condemned to death with his two companions. The sentence was to be carried out the next day, at St. Mary's Bridge, in Derbyshire.

Henry Garnet, cited in Sweeney, recounts that the priests spent their last night in the same cell as a woman condemned to death for murder, and that in the course of the night, they reconciled her to the Catholic Faith, and she was hanged with them the next day.

On 24th July 1588, the three priests were drawn on hurdles to the place of execution, where they were hanged, drawn, and quartered. Simpson was apparently to have been executed first, but reports state that Garlick hastened to the ladder before him and kissed it, going up first, either because, as suggested by Anthony Champney, Simpson was showing some signs of fear, or, as suggested by Challoner, Garlick suspected that there was a danger that his companion's courage might fail him. Simpson was next to die, and an eyewitness, quoted in Challoner, said that he "suffered with great constancy, though not with such (remarkable) signs of joy and alacrity as the other two." When his body was cut down for quartering, he was found to be wearing a hairshirt. Another eyewitness, quoted in Hayward, says:

"What he said to his executioner I cannot hear, but embracing the ladder he kissed the steps. When he was in quartering, the people cried out, 'A devil, a devil,' because he had on him a shirt of hair; but the wiser sort said he wore it because he had fallen."

A poem by an anonymous writer, who seems to have been present at the executions, and is quoted in Challoner, describes the executions as follows:

When Garlick did the ladder kiss,
And Sympson after hie,

Methought that there St. Andrew was
Desirous for to die.

When Ludlam lookèd smilingly,
And joyful did remain,
It seemed St. Stephen was standing by,
For to be stoned again.

And what if Sympson seemed to yield,
For doubt and dread to die;
He rose again, and won the field
And died most constantly.

His watching, fasting, shirt of hair;
His speech, his death, and all,
Do record give, do witness bear,
He wailed his former fall.

Blessed Peter Snow

Born at Ripon, Yorkshire
Martyred at York, 15th June, 1598 under Elizabeth I
Beatified on 22nd November, 1997
by Pope St John Paul II

Peter Snow arrived at the English College, Rheims, on 17th April 1589. He was ordained to the priesthood at Soissons in March 1591.

Snow left for England on the following 15th May. He was arrested about 1st May 1598, when on his way to York with Blessed Ralph Grimston of Nidd. Both were shortly after condemned, Snow of treason as being a priest and Grimston of felony, for having aided and assisted him, and, it is said, having attempted to prevent his apprehension. They were martyred in York on the Knavesmire on 15th June 1598. Afterwards their severed heads were impaled on spikes and exposed in the town as a warning to all.

In 1845, two skulls were discovered under the stone floor of the ancient chapel of Hazlewood Castle, near Tadcaster. At the time they were thought to be relics of two other English martyrs, John Lockwood and Edmund Catherick and the skulls were placed in a niche near the altar. In 1909, it was discovered that they were the relics of Peter Snow and Ralph Grimston.

In 2005, Rt Revd Arthur Roche, Bishop of Leeds, decided to place the relics in Leeds Cathedral altar. He ordered reconstruction of their faces using the latest techniques from the University of Dundee.

Blessed William Spenser

Born at York
Martyred at York, 24th September, 1589
under Elizabeth I
Beatified on 22nd November, 1987
by Pope St John Paul II

William Spenser was born in the Craven district of York, but educated by his maternal uncle, who had been ordained priest in the reign of Queen Mary, at his living at Chipping Norton, Oxfordshire. Spenser then entered Trinity College, Oxford, going on to become a fellow of the same college, which had the honour to produce no fewer than five beatified martyrs.

Spenser became convinced of the truth of the Catholic faith, and struggled with his conscience for two years before going to Rheims, where he was ordained priest and then returned to England in 1584. He went to Yorkshire and met his parents in a field, disguised as a labourer, and brought about their conversion. His uncle too, Blessed William persuaded to leave the comfort of Chipping Norton and to make his home with a Catholic family. Spenser hid in the home of Blessed Robert Hardesty and then devoted himself to the care of Catholic prisoners in York Castle, even hiding with them within the castle walls. He was arrested when on a journey, and suffered the torments of his execution with great fortitude.

Blessed Edmund Sykes

Born at Leeds
Martyred at York, 23rd March, 1587 under Elizabeth I
Beatified on 22nd November, 1987
by Pope St John Paul II

Edmund Sykes was ordained at the English College in Rheims on 21st February, 1581 and then sent on the English Mission on 5th June. He laboured for souls in Yorkshire for around three years, before being worn out by his work and then confining himself to Leeds. An apostate Catholic, Arthur Webster, betrayed him and Sykes was imprisoned in the ghastly Ousebridge Kidcote in York by the Council of the North. Under pressure, he once attended a Protestant service, but repented of this weakness and so was imprisoned for a further six months. The Council then sentenced him to banishment, and so he was transferred to Hull Castle before being shipped overseas.

On being deported, Sykes went to Rome and stayed at the English College for nine days in April 1586. His pilgrimage strengthened his resolve to return to the English Mission in atonement for his brief lapse, and he was back in England in June 1586. After staying at his brother's house at Wath in the West Riding, the brother betrayed him, and Sykes was detained at York Castle, before being brought before the Lent Assizes and condemned as a traitor on account of his priesthood. He was dragged on the hurdle from the Castle to York Tyburn, where he was hanged, drawn and quartered.

Blessed John Talbot

Born at Thornton-le-Street, Yorkshire
Martyred at Durham, 9th August, 1600 under Elizabeth I
Beatified on 22nd November, 1987
by Pope St John Paul II

John Talbot had already been persecuted for his adherence to the Catholic faith, having been convicted of recusancy in 1588.

As a result of his faith, Blessed John Talbot suffered severe persecution, including multiple arrests, fines and confiscation of his property. He had to endure these punishments on a daily basis - a severe test of his faith and loyalty.

John Talbot was present at prayer with the priest, Blessed Thomas Palasor, Blessed John Norton and several companions at a house in Lamesley, Gateshead when he was arrested in 1600. It was Mr Talbot who tried to prevent the arrest of the priest. For this, he too was arrested as a traitor.

Talbot was imprisoned and confined in a dungeon and shortly thereafter, sentenced to be hanged, drawn and quartered for the crime of harbouring a Catholic priest. On Wednesday 9th August 1600, Blessed John Talbot was brought to the gallows site in Durham, on the crest of the hill at the north side of Durham City. He was given the chance to save his life if he would renounce the Catholic faith and attend Protestant services; he refused. Talbot was tortured on the rack, hanged until not quite dead, then disembowelled, before being beheaded.

Blessed Hugh Taylor

Born at Durham
Martyred at York, 25th November, 1585
under Elizabeth I
Beatified on 22nd November, 1987
by Pope St John Paul II

Not much is known about Blessed Hugh Taylor, but he was the first martyr to be executed under the Statute 27 Eliz. C. 2, which made it treason to be made a priest and then to come into the realm. Taylor arrived at Rheims on 2nd May 1582 and was sent on the English mission on 27th March 1585. After a few months he was apprehended. The layman Blessed Marmaduke Bowes, was arrested for having harboured this priest. They were executed on the same occasion, Hugh Taylor being hanged, drawn and quartered.

Blessed Richard Thirkeld

Born at Coniscliffe, Durham
Martyred at York, 29th May, 1583 under Elizabeth I
Beatified on 29th December, 1886 by Pope Leo XIII

Richard Thirkeld was an undergraduate at the Queen's College, Oxford from 1564-5 but left for Rheims, France, where he was later ordained priest on 18th April 1879. He left on 23rd May for England, where his priestly ministry was based in or around York. He was confessor to St Margaret Clitherow.

On the eve of the Annunciation 1583 Blessed Richard went to visit one of the Catholic prisoners at the Kidcote Prison on the Ouse Bridge. He was arrested and immediately confessed his priesthood to the pursuivants and then to the Lord Mayor of York. After being held in the house of the High Sherriff overnight, Thirkeld managed to appear the next day in court wearing a cassock and biretta. He was charged with having reconciled the Queen's subjects to the Church of Rome, found guilty on 27th May and condemned on 28th May.

On the night before his execution Blessed Richard spent his time instructing and encouraging other Catholic prisoners. He was hanged, drawn and quartered privately, for fear of a disturbance. Six of his letters survive.

Blessed James Thompson

Born at York
Martyred at York, 28th November, 1582
under Elizabeth I
Beatified on 29th December, 1886 by Pope Leo XIII

Blessed James Thompson, also known as James Hudson, was a native of York and arrived at Dr Allen's college at Rheims on 19th September, 1580, and in May of the next year, by virtue of a dispensation, was admitted at Soissons, with one Nicholas Fox, to all sacred orders within twelve days, although at the time he was so ill that he could hardly stand.

Thompson was sent on the mission the following 10th August, and was arrested at York on 11th August, 1582. On being taken before the Council of the North he frankly confessed his priesthood, to the astonishment of his fellow citizens who knew that he had not been away more than a year. He was then loaded with double irons and was imprisoned, first in a private gaol, till his money was exhausted, and then in York Castle. On 25th November he was brought to the bar and condemned to the penalties of high treason. He suffered with great joy and tranquility at the Knavesmire, protesting that he had never plotted against the Queen, and that he died in and for the Catholic faith. While he was hanging, he first raised his hands to heaven, then beat his breast with his right hand, and finally made a great sign of the cross. In spite of his sentence, he was neither disembowelled nor quartered, but was buried under the gallows.

Blessed Robert Thorpe

Born in Yorkshire, c.1560
Martyred at York, 31st May, 1591 under Elizabeth I
Beatified on 22nd November, 1987,
by Pope St John Paul II

Robert Thorpe (or Thorp) studied at the English College in Rheims and was ordained priest before returning to his native Yorkshire in May 1585. He laboured there for souls until the eve of Palm Sunday 1591, when a neighbour of Blessed Thomas Watkinson spotted palms being prepared and deduced that a priest must have been in the house. The Justice of the Peace was informed and brought a company very early the next morning, so that both Robert Thorpe and Thomas Watkinson were carried off from their beds.

Both were condemned and then hanged, drawn and quartered at York.

Blessed Edward Thwing

Born at Heworth, York, c.1565
Martyred at Lancaster, 26th July, 1600 under Elizabeth I
Beatified on 22nd November, 1987
by Pope St John Paul II

Edward Thwing was the second son of Thomas Thwing of Heworth, York and Jane (née Kellet, of York), his wife. He was related to the fourteenth century saint John Thwing of Bridlington.

Thwing went to the English College at Rheims in the summer of 1583. Then he spent some time with the Jesuits at Pont-à-Mousson. He returned to Rheims in July 1585, where he remained until September 1587. He then went to Rome to complete his studies. He returned to Reims because of ill health and became a reader in Greek and Hebrew, and a professor of rhetoric and logic. He was ordained priest at Laon in December 1590. In November 1592, he went to Spa suffering from an ulcer in the knee. He returned to the English College, which had in the meantime been transferred from Rheims to Douai.

Thwing was sent on the English mission in 1597. He seems to have been immediately arrested and charged under the Jesuits, etc. Act 1584, ("An act against Jesuits, seminary priests, and such other like disobedient persons") (27 Eliz.1, c. 2). The Act commanded all Roman Catholic priests to leave the country in forty days or they would be punished for high treason, unless within the forty days they swore an oath to obey the Queen. Those who harboured them, and all those who knew of their presence and failed to inform the authorities would be fined and imprisoned for felony. He and Dominican friar Robert Nutter were sent to Wisbech Castle, a state ecclesiastical prison. The area of Wisbech was an important centre for English Catholicism. The castle's residents were supported by Catholic alms and were relatively comfortable. Henry Garnet reported that the keeper would allow detainees permission to move within a five-mile radius.

Thwing and Nutter escaped to Lancashire and eluded capture for three years. They were arrested again in May 1600 and were committed to Lancaster Castle, tried at the next assizes and condemned for being priests. Thwing was hanged, drawn, and quartered at Lancaster, along with Robert Nutter on 26th July 1600. Thwing's great-nephew, Blessed Thomas Thwing suffered the same fate in 1680 for his supposed part in the Barnbow Plot, an offshoot of the fabricated Popish Plot invented by Titus Oates.

Blessed Thomas Thwing

Born at Heworth Hall, Yorkshire, 1635
Martyred at York, 23rd October, 1680 under Charles II
Beatified on 15th December, 1929 by Pope Pius XI

Thomas Thwing's father was George Thwing, Esq. of Kilton Castle, Brotton, and Heworth Hall. His mother was

Anne, daughter of Sir John Gascoigne and his wife Anne Ingleby, and sister of Sir Thomas Gascoigne, 2nd Baronet, of Barnbow Hall, Barwick in Elmet. Both parents were Yorkshire recusants. The martyr Blessed Edward Thwing was his great-uncle, and he is also related to the fourteenth-century Saint John of Bridlington.

Thomas was educated at St Omer and at the English College, Douai, ordained a priest and sent to minister at the English Mission in 1665, which he did for roughly fourteen years. Until April 1668, he was chaplain at Carlton Hall, the seat of his cousins, the Stapleton family. He opened a school at Quosque, the Stapletons' dower-house. He lived on Hepworth Lane, in Carlton, Selby.

In 1677 Mary Ward's Institute of the Blessed Virgin Mary began its foundation in the house given to the order by Thomas' maternal uncle, Thomas Gascoigne, at Dolebank, where three of Father Thwing's sisters were members. Thwing became chaplain and it was there that he was arrested in early 1679.

At the time of the Titus Oates scare, or 'Popish Plot', two servants, Bolron and Mowbray, who had been discharged from Sir Thomas Gascoigne's service for dishonesty, sought vengeance and reward by revealing a supposed plot by Gascoigne and others to murder King Charles II. At first the informers made no mention of Thwing. Nevertheless, Gascoigne, his daughter Lady Tempest, Thwing, and others were arrested on the night of 7th July 1679, and removed to London for trial at Newgate.

Gascoigne sensibly demanded to be tried by a Yorkshire jury, whom the judges admitted were better equipped to decide on the credibility of witnesses, most of whom they knew personally, than were the judges themselves. The trial was postponed to the summer assizes. Thwing was brought to the bar on 29th July, and Gascoigne's former servant, Robert Bolron, testified against him. All of the accused were acquitted except Thwing, who was brought back to York, where he was arraigned at York on 17th March 1680, along with, among others, a kinsman, Sir Miles Stapleton. The prosecution played upon a list of Catholics which had been found on the night of the arrest. In reality they were not conspirators but supporters of the new convent at Dolebank which Gascoigne's daughter Lady Tempest had recently founded. At her father's trial the Court had heard much evidence about the convent, but the judges apparently did not regard her actions as treasonable, since at her own trial she was acquitted. Sir Miles Stapleton was also acquitted, as was another alleged conspirator, Mary Pressicks: the judges, showing far more impartiality than in earlier Popish Plot trials, ruled that her statement that "we shall never be at peace till we are all of the Roman Catholic faith" was not treasonable, but a simple expression of opinion.

Despite the acquittal of Stapleton and Mrs. Pressicks, Thwing was promptly found guilty on the very same evidence upon which his relatives had been acquitted. Upon hearing the sentence, he humbly bowed his head, saying in Latin, "Innocens ego sum" (I am innocent).

The King at first reprieved him, but owing to a remonstrance of the Commons the death-warrant was issued on the day after the meeting of Parliament. Thwing was hanged, drawn, and quartered at the Tyburn in York on 23rd October, 1680. His friends interred his quartered body.

There is a statue of Blessed Thomas Thwing in the shrine of St Margaret Clitherow on the Shambles. He is the last of the York martyrs.

Saint Henry Walpole

Born at Docking, Norfolk, 1588
Martyred at York, 7th April, 1595 under Elizabeth I
Beatified on 15th December, 1929 by Pope Pius XI
Canonized on 25th October, 1970 by Pope St Paul VI

Saint Henry Walpole was educated at Norwich School and Peterhouse, Cambridge, before reading for the Bar at Gray's Inn, where he came to the attention of government spies for his frequent association with recusant gentry. Walpole was present at the disputes held between St Edmund Campion and Protestant theologians and then at Campion's execution in 1581. When St Henry's clothes were sprinkled with the martyred Jesuit's blood he experienced a call to conversion, gave up his law practice and devoted himself to the Catholic religion. He wrote a volume of poems in honour of Edmund Campion, which was secretly printed and circulated in London. The printer, a friend of Walpole called Valenger, was fined and had his ears cut off, but he did not betray the author of the verses. Walpole fled home to Norfolk, and then escaped to France.

In 1583 Henry Walpole was admitted to the English College in Rome, where he received minor orders. The following year he joined the Society of Jesus and continued his studies at the Scots College at Pont-à-Mousson. He was ordained sub-deacon and deacon at Metz, and then made a priest at Paris on 17th December 1588.

Walpole was highly talented: he was fluent in Italian, French, English, Latin and Spanish. After a year in Brussels he was appointed chaplain to English and Irish refugees serving in the Spanish army in the Netherlands. The English captured him and took him to their fort at Flushing, where he was tortured, but then ransomed by his brother Michael and the Jesuit superiors. Walpole then performed his Jesuit tertianship at Tournai, before assisting with the foundation of the English colleges at Seville and Valladolid. In 1593 he went to ask King Philip II of Spain for permission to found the college at St Omer (now Stonyhurst).

Walpole, his youngest brother Thomas, and an English soldier sailed from Dunkirk on a French ship headed for Scotland because the southern ports of England were closed on account of the plague. After ten days of stormy seas, they were put ashore at Flamborough Head, Yorkshire, on 4th December 1593, and immediately split up. Walpole was arrested at an inn at Bridlington, having been betrayed by a fellow passenger, who was earning money to buy his way out of prison. Walpole was imprisoned for the next sixteen months.

He spent about three months at York Castle before the notorious priest-hunter Richard Topcliffe had Walpole transferred to the Tower of London in February 1594. There Walpole was tortured on the rack and suspended by his wrists for hours. Fourteen sessions were spaced out so as not to cause his accidental death under interrogation. His father was in failing health, and as his heir, if Henry was subsequently condemned for treason, the estate would all go to the Crown.

While incarcerated in the Salt Tower, Fr Walpole carved his name in the plaster along with those of saints Peter, Paul, Jerome, Ambrose, Augustine, and Gregory the Great.

In the spring of 1595 he was sent back to York for trial, where he was joined by Alexander Rawlins, who was also awaiting trial. Both were tried on 3rd April on the charge of being Catholic priests. Walpole, a former lawyer, argued that the law only applied to priests who had not given themselves up to officials within three days of arrival. He himself had been arrested less than a day after landing in England, so he had not violated that law. The judges demanded that he take the Oath of Supremacy, acknowledging the Queen's complete authority in religion. He refused to do so and was convicted of high treason. Both he and Rawlins were found guilty and condemned and on 7th April 1595 they were hanged, drawn and quartered. Rawlins died first; Walpole was allowed to hang until he was dead.

Blessed James Walworth

Martyred at York, 11th May, 1537 under Henry VIII
Beatified on 29th December, 1886 by Pope Leo XIII

Along with Blessed John Rochester, James Walworth was the first to be executed for the faith during the period of persecution in York. We know nothing about his early life, but that he was a monk of the London Charterhouse. In May 1535, three English Carthusians became the first martyrs of the reformation when they were executed at Tyburn for refusing to agree to the royal supremacy over the Church. Three more monks of the London Charterhouse followed in

June – in the end fifteen members of that illustrious community were to be martyred. Dom James was one of the monks who was taken to other Carthusian houses, in his case to the Charterhouse of St Michael in Hull.

After the Pilgrimage of Grace in October 1536, Dom John Rochester and Dom James Walworth were brought to York to stand trial for treason before the Duke of Norfolk, Lord President of the Council of the North. On 11th May 1537 the two monks became the first martyrs to suffer in York when they were publicly hanged until death by exposure and dehydration, and their bodies then hung in chains from the city battlements.

Blessed Thomas Warcop

Born in Yorkshire
Martyred at York, 4th July, 1597 under Elizabeth I
Beatified on 15th December, 1929 by Pope Pius XI

Blessed Thomas Warcop was a Yorkshire gentleman, who harboured the priest Blessed William Andleby in his house, and for this was condemned to die the death of a traitor with him in York on 4th July 1597.

Blessed Robert Watkinson

Born at Hemingborough, Yorkshire, 1579
Martyred at York, 20th April, 1602, under James I
Beatified on 15th December, 1929 by Pope Pius XI

Robert Watkinson was educated at Douay and Rome and then ordained priest at Arras on 25th March 1602. When in London, under the care of a doctor, he was betrayed by John Fewether, apprehended, arraigned, and condemned.

Challoner recounts this story about Mr Watkinson, that the day before his arrest, as he was walking in the London streets with another Catholic, he met a stranger with the appearance of a venerable old man, who saluted him with these words: "Jesus bless you, you seem to be sick and troubled with many infirmities; but be of good cheer; for within these four days you shall be cured of all." He was indeed executed four days later.

On the morning of his execution, Robert Watkinson found means to celebrate Mass in prison, served by Mr Henry Owen., who perceived about his head, sometimes on the one side, sometimes on the other, a most bright light, like a ray of glory; which, from the consecration till after the Communion, rested directly over his head, and then disappeared.

Blessed Thomas Watkinson

Born in Yorkshire
Martyred at York, 31st May, 1591 under Elizabeth I
Beatified on 22nd November, 1987
by Pope St John Paul II

A native of Yorkshire, England, Thomas Watkinson was a devout Catholic widower who became a cleric (evidently receiving minor orders, not the diaconate or the priesthood). He lived in solitude, but took an active role in assisting and sheltering the priests who secretly served the country's Catholics persecuted under Queen Elizabeth I.

On the eve of Palm Sunday in 1591, a hostile neighbour of Watkinson spotted the widower's servants procuring palms. This "incriminating evidence" was reported to a magistrate three miles away. Very early on Palm Sunday morning, the magistrate raided Watkinson's home, arresting the widower and Robert Thorpe, the priest who had come to celebrate Mass. They were sent to London, where they were tortured by the murderous government agent Richard Topcliffe.

After being returned to York, Thorpe was sentenced to drawing and quartering for his priesthood, and Watkinson was sentenced to hanging for having sheltered priests. Watkinson was offered his life if he agreed to attend Protestant church services, but he refused. On 31st May 1591, both men suffered death with great courage.

Blessed Thomas Welbourne

Born at Kitenbushell, Yorkshire
Martyred at York, 1st August, 1605 under James I
Beatified on 15th December, 1929 by Pope Pius XI

Thomas Welbourne was a schoolmaster, who along with another zealous Catholic, John Fulthering, exhorted their neighbours to embrace the Catholic faith. In consequence the two of them were convicted of high treason and executed at York on 1st August 1605.

Blessed Christopher Wharton

Born at Middleton, Yorkshire, c.1546
Martyred at York, 28th March, 1600 under Elizabeth I
Beatified on 22nd November, 1987
by Pope St John Paul II

Christopher Wharton was the second son of Sir Thomas Wharton of Wharton and Agnes Warcop, and younger brother of Thomas Wharton, first Baron Wharton. He was educated at Trinity College, Oxford, where he graduated MA in February 1564, and afterwards became a Fellow. During his time at Oxford, he converted to Catholicism.

In 1583 Wharton left England and entered the English College at Rheims to study for the priesthood He was ordained priest in the following year, but continued his studies after ordination till 1586, when on 21st May he left Rheims in company with Blessed Edward Burden, whom he had known from his days at Trinity.

No details of Wharton's missionary work have been preserved; but at his trial Baron Savile, the judge, incidentally remarked that he had known him at Oxford some years after 1596. He was finally arrested in 1599 at the house of Eleanor Hunt, a widow, who was arrested with him and confined in York Castle. There, with other Catholic prisoners, he was forcibly taken to hear Protestant sermons. He was brought to trial together with Mrs Hunt at the Lent Assizes 1600, and both were condemned, the former for high treason, the latter for felony. Both refused life and liberty at the price of conformity. Wharton was executed; Eleanor Hunt died in prison.

Wharton's severed head was put on one of the gates of York, but was rescued by Catholics, who kept it safe in Knaresborough. It was then taken into safe keeping by the Benedictines at Downside, who later returned it to the Catholics of Leeds.

Afterword

In addition to the small biographies here, there are another 43 names of those who suffered for the faith and who either died in prison, or about whom too little is known. They are listed below, and bring the total of York martyrs to at least 128:

12 priests, who died in prison in York on unknown dates:

John Ackridge,
William Baldwin,
William Bannersley,
Thomas Bedel,
Richard Bowes,
Henry Comberford,
James Gerard,
Nicholas Grene,
Thomas Harwood,
John Pearson,
Thomas Riddal,
James Swarbrick.

31 lay men and women, who died in prison:

Anthony Ash,
Thomas Blenkinsop,
Stephen Branton,
Lucy Budge,
John Chalmar,
Isabel Chalmar,
John Constable,

Ralph Cowling,
John Eldersha,
Isabel Foster,
Mr Foster,
Agnes Fuister,
Thomas Horsley,
Stephen Hemsworth,
Mary Hutton,
Agnes Johnson,
Thomas Layne,
Thomas Luke,
Alice Oldcorne,
Mr Reynold,
Mr Robinson,
John Stable,
Margaret Stable,
Geoffrey Stephenson,
Thomas Vavasour,
Dorothy Vavasour,
Margaret Webster,
Frances Webster,
Christopher Watson,
Hercules Welbourne,
Alice Williamson.

In reflecting on this glorious array of local martyrs we should remember those countless Christians around the world today who suffer for their faith. The blood of the martyrs is the seed of the Church. May the witness of the martyrs and confessors of all ages bear fruit in a new springtime of faith.

All you holy martyrs of York – pray for us.